The Secrets of Big Business Innovation

Dan Taylor is managing director of the New York office of Market Gravity, an innovation consultancy that works with the world's best companies to identify, develop and deliver new propositions and services. Dan has been at the frontline of corporate innovation for over 15 years, working in and with some of the world's largest companies to establish and sustain innovation.

Dan has developed and launched everything from digital payments ventures to engineering businesses, from smart home technologies to electric vehicle businesses, and from media ventures to telecoms tariffs. He has also founded some of his own businesses along the way. In a clear and punchy way, Dan brings to life the challenges of corporate innovation and the secrets of success.

Daniel Taylor

The Secrets of Big Business Innovation

An insider's guide to delivering innovation, change and growth

Harriman House

HARRIMAN HOUSE LTD
18 College Street
Petersfield
Hampshire
GU31 4AD
GREAT BRITAIN
Tel: +44 (0)1730 233870
Email: contact@harriman-house.com
Website: www.harriman-house.com

First published in Great Britain in 2015
Black and white edition, 2017

Paperback ISBN: 9780857194640
eBook ISBN: 9780857194824

British Library Cataloguing in Publication Data
A CIP catalogue record for this book can be obtained from the British Library.

Contents

Introduction

Every owner of a physical copy of

The Secrets of Big Business Innovation

can download the eBook for free direct from us
at Harriman House, in a format that can be read
on any eReader, tablet or smartphone.

Simply head to:

ebooks.harriman-house.com/businessinnovation

to get your copy now.

Corporate entrepreneurs or intrapreneurs

The focus of this book is the work of corporate entrepreneurs or *intrapreneurs.* These people work in large corporates, tasked with delivering new offerings to customers. They drive innovation, change and growth in corporations all over the world by launching new products and services into adjacent, new or emerging markets with new customers, technologies and business models. They can often be found in functions such as the new product development team, developing new product extensions, an innovation team developing more step-change ideas, the research & development function, which focuses on developing new technologies or intellectual property, and also in the corporate venture capital function, which invests in start-ups to drive growth. This book contains insights and anecdotes from executives and practitioners across all of these functions.

I have written this insider's guide for those on the ground, whether leaders, team members, sponsors, stakeholders or even external advisors. The focus is on presenting practical experience and advice from experts who face the challenges of corporate innovation every day.

Big business innovation is important

For some companies – like Google and Apple – innovation is at the core of everything they do, but even for more traditional companies in historically slower moving industries, innovation can be the difference between growing and declining, between surviving and dying. For example, there are now three famous examples from the photographic industry of large companies going bankrupt due to a failure to innovate.

First, Kodak famously chose to invest in improving its film technology rather than pursuing the digital photography market, despite having invented digital photography back in 1975. Polaroid suffered a similar fate and filed for bankruptcy in 2001. Then Jessops, the market-leading retailer of cameras and film processing in the UK, went bankrupt after failing to adapt to the growth of e-retail and the implications of digital cameras. Many critics think of innovation as risky, but in fact it is often far more risky not to innovate, especially when innovation is done well.

Clearly, the photographic industry is just one example. Every industry is facing change and new technologies, new connectivity and new business models mean this change is coming faster than ever. This in turn drives a need not just to innovate, but to innovate more quickly and more flexibly than ever before. Every organisation in every sector can benefit from innovation, although too many only realise this when they are starting to decline, rather than using innovation as a proactive driver of sustainable growth. Innovation can drive softer benefits too, from better brand perception to improved recruitment and retention of talent across the organisation, and even a higher market valuation.

Furthermore, big businesses often have significant assets, such as brand, infrastructure or a customer base, that create an advantage in the market and can be leveraged successfully, as evidenced by the British Telecom example below. So innovation is not only important to both the survival and growth of large organisations, but they also tend to have advantages that can enable them, in theory at least, to be successful at it.

> ## Case example: Leveraging corporate assets – OpenZone at BT
>
> When at BT, I launched OpenZone, the first Wi-Fi network in the UK. The truth is that it would have been nothing without BT. We were a mobile product team and BT had just launched broadband. Wi-Fi was already in the USA, so we replicated the technology for the UK market. Because of BT's size and assets, they could make it happen when nobody else could. It was a fantastically strong product and with BT's assets we were able to rollout nationwide, and we could not have gone so quickly if we were not BT.
>
> **Sandrine Desbarbieux, Former Head of Marketing at British Telecom**

Big business innovation is hard

However, where optimism around innovation exists it is common for it not to be backed up with sustained action. As we shall see later, a lack of commitment to leveraging those assets I mentioned above means one of the key advantages of the business is not exploited and the project is ruined.

While innovation is hard for start-ups, who have to identify a market opportunity, create a proposition that will address that opportunity and then execute it, it can be even harder for large organisations, who not only have to do these things, but also have to contend with myriad internal challenges such as corporate governance and process, managing stakeholders, and maintaining focus and commitment to the innovation programme when there are so many other important things going on inside the business.

Many big businesses that try to innovate find the different ways of working, the level of uncertainty and risk, and ultimately the ability to execute, incredibly difficult. This may lead to failure, or more commonly perceived failure, as they mistakenly compare themselves to Apple or Google. The truth is that for every successful venture out there, whether at Google or just a small start-up, there are hundreds of failures littered at the wayside. The reality of this success rate sits outside the standard parameters for most big companies that have spent many years focusing on doing a few things very well to succeed in their industry. And so the innovation programme comes to an end, even when it may have been performing well.

Such failure is often blamed on poor execution, internal politics or bureaucracy, but all of these are symptoms of the way the innovation programme is established and delivered. In this book, I seek to expose the root causes of these challenges and provide a range of case examples to demonstrate how others have approached them.

Innovation is evolving

New technology is enabling rapid advances in innovation, not just in the products and services themselves, but also in the way in which innovation is delivered. Rapid prototyping platforms, 3D printing and lean start-up principles are all contributing to faster delivery, more flexible approaches and rapidly evolving processes. These all enable improvements to innovation in big businesses, but it is still important to hang on to many of the underlying practices that have always enabled successful innovation in the corporate environment. It can be easy in a world of 3D printed prototyping to ignore these traditional secrets of success, yet as highlighted in many of the case examples in this book, they remain as important as ever.

Practical guidance and examples

There are countless books and papers on the topic of innovation, but I have never found one that actually corresponds to the reality of being on the ground inside a corporate innovation programme. Instead, they are typically stuck in a world of academic theory and high-level strategy, trying to address start-up rather than corporate challenges, or are focused on selling the solution of whichever consultancy or guru is writing it.

Therefore, I am not going to discuss how to build a new product or position it in the market, nor the strategic role of innovation within a business, nor do I promote a single approach, as I don't believe there is a single answer. Instead, I highlight a range of different ways to overcome the common challenges and deliver innovation projects within big businesses.

The book contains over 100 case examples and comments from interviews with top corporate entrepreneurs, innovation experts and practitioners around the world, spanning a wide range of businesses. These men and women have great experience, usually from learning the hard way, and all of them have provided a wealth of knowledge, insight and experience of where innovation goes right and wrong. I hope you can benefit from it as I have.

Practising what I preach – a limited edition

Whilst writing this book, I tried to practise what I preach by following the principles set out within it. To that end, I spoke with many intrapreneurs to understand what they would like to gain from a book of this nature, and whether they would buy it and/or read it. I solicited feedback on the text from editors and experts as well as friends and family. However, as explained in chapter 7, the only way to find out the truth is to try to sell it for real. So, as recommended in the book, *The Secrets of Big Business Innovation* was originally published as a limited, colour edition. You are now reading the subsequent print run of the book, a black and white edition. Please give feedback and submit your own experiences to me via my About Me page (about.me/Dan.T.Taylor).

The innovation framework

This book's structure is based on an innovation framework that is comprised of three equally important sections:

A. Establishing an innovation programme: Understanding the purpose of innovation and putting in place the right governance, leadership, structure, frameworks, people and culture.

B. Delivering innovation projects: Identifying, developing and launching new products and services.

C. Sustaining innovation: Scaling new products, managing the portfolio of existing products and those in development, and working with the core business to make the most of the programme and give it a lasting impact.

Typically, successful and sustainable innovation programmes in big businesses have properly considered all three of the elements within the framework and acknowledged that the three are interrelated and interdependent. Just because an individual innovation project goes well, it does not mean that the overall programme will be successful or sustainable. Likewise, the factors that cause an innovation project to struggle are just as likely to sit in the way the overall programme is established as within the individual project.

Figure I.1 presents an illustration of the innovation framework.

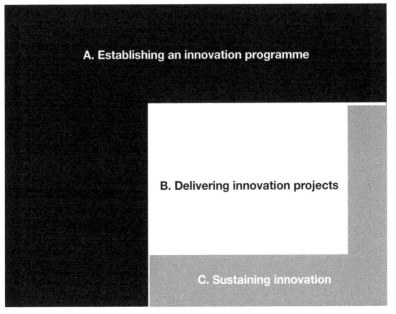

Figure I.1: Innovation framework

Establishing An Innovation Programme

Section A

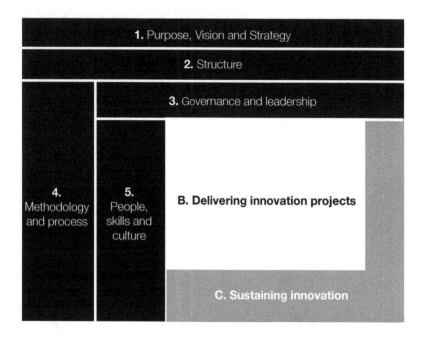

Figure A.1: Innovation framework

Many of the challenges facing individual innovation projects have their root causes in how the overall programme is set up. This can include governance or structure, the methodology and processes employed, the team's skill set and culture, and even the purpose of establishing the programme in the first place. Therefore, careful consideration needs to be given to how an innovation programme is established long before any individual ideas are looked at.

Figure A.1 shows a modified version of the innovation framework diagram, with section A on establishing innovation broken down into its principal constituent areas.

The chapters of Section A discuss these sub-sections within establishing innovation.

1. Purpose, Vision and Strategy

The first step when establishing innovation is to clarify the purpose and goals of innovation and the level of commitment.

Innovation is an important lever for sustaining growth in any organisation, but there can be a wide variety of reasons why a company invests in innovation. For some companies, Samsung and Apple for example, it is the core of what they do. For others, it may be seen as an escape mechanism if the core business is in trouble. Others see it as fashionable and hope that maybe they could be the next Apple, some do it because they need something to tell their investors to defend the share price, others use it to try to improve employee engagement, or of course, it can be part of an ongoing balanced growth strategy.

Clearly understand the purpose

Innovation takes time and will require an ongoing commitment from the business to be successful. For this to be realised, a strong rationale is required so that the business has little choice but to innovate. This can be as extreme as declining revenues and profits in the core business, or a regulatory enforced change, but sometimes a slowed growth rate or even, as in the case of comparethemarket. com below, the fear of market changes can be enough to make the core business face the fact that cost-cutting isn't enough and that it has to adapt its offer to the evolving marketplace.

Case example: Preparing for the future at comparethemarket.com

At comparethemarket.com, things are going well but you need to be ready for trouble. It's not our known competitors that scare me. It's the kids in their parents' garage that hack something together and totally disrupt the entire category. We've agreed the brand vision and are now innovating towards it. Innovation is fundamental to the future of the brand. Innovation to us is an emotive, purposeful, and significant leap towards the new brand experience. If you suffocate this, then you suffocate the future of the company.

Benjamin Braun, Associate Director at comparethemarket.com

Understanding this underlying driver of the overall programme will give a clear focus for the programme and offer a clue as to which projects are likely to be successful, whether it be a focus on process efficiencies, reducing churn, acquiring new customers or entering new markets. This clarity of purpose needs setting out both as the context for the programme but also to inform its vision and strategy.

A burning platform

Programmes that lack a burning platform, or the fear of a burning platform, have limited chance of success. As the former head of design at Virgin Atlantic puts it:

> "Burning platforms with a strong case for change are the best way to get most companies investing in innovation. If you're looking down the barrel, then you have to come up with something better than the competition. That focuses the mind and brings budget, resource, focus and a sense of urgency to actually go beyond the day to day."

Joe Ferry, former head of design, Virgin Atlantic

A range of potential reasons for embarking on an innovation programme are highlighted above, and those that are not genuinely critical to business survival will typically have a far shorter window to prove their worth to the business than those that have a true *burning platform*. Those programmes without such a business-critical purpose typically struggle to maintain support and focus and eventually die.

The strongest purpose for innovation is one that contains some kind of burning platform, which most often comes in the form of competition, or the regulator in some industries. Competition pulls deep psychological strings and when combined with missed growth targets or a dwindling customer base, it can be a powerful motivator for change. There are a few case examples in this book that cover innovation at British Airways and Virgin Atlantic, and it is clear that both were driven to invest by their battle against each other to win the key business class market.

However, whilst such a rationale needs to be clear and understood, it is most effective when counterbalanced by an ambitious vision that turns a depressing "do or die" message into an inspirational rallying cry. Around this, support can be garnered for setting off in a challenging, yet clear, direction. When there is a burning platform, ideally combined with broad strategic objectives and vision for change, then the chances of success are far greater, as demonstrated by the O2/giffgaff example below.

Case example: Slowing growth created the focus for new venture at O2

I was at O2, and giffgaff came about after I fought for the need to have someone in my team with no real job description other than to find good ideas. It was hard to get buy-in to this and at the budget round the other directors challenged it saying they could employ ten customer service agents for the cost of this one person – but I defended it on the basis that if we did that it'd be the same old O2. Big organisations have to protect bandwidth to enable it to happen. Over-cost cutting will engineer out opportunities for left-field thinking.

But the board saw we had to do this, they had recognised a lack of innovation and that there was nothing new or new revenue streams coming through. Growth was slowing in our main mass market propositions and so appetite was there for innovation and something new.

So I got this person, and he soon came back from a web 2.0 conference in San Francisco with an idea of what would web 2.0 mean for a mobile operator – run by the customers, with no call centre, and self-determining a whole list of principles. Then the ad agency mocked up a video to get buy-in which really worked and most importantly it ticked the box strategically – it meant going after more niche segments to drive growth in a new way and was complementary rather than substitutional to the main business. giffgaff, which now has over a million customers under a different brand, was born.

Tim Sefton, Former Business Development Director, O2

Commit to innovation and understand its implications

Sometimes it is easy to sit in a meeting and agree that innovation is important, support its purpose, and even sign off investment into it, without really understanding the full implications. As we know, innovation is hard and it requires patience, focus and investment to succeed. Ensuring that the leadership has the right level of understanding and commitment to see it through can be critical to success. This is illustrated by the example of Ashland below.

Case example: Clarifying the purpose and commitment with the CEO at Ashland

You have to understand the focus of the President and the CEO is to balance the short and long-term investments required to grow the business. Innovation definitely can play a role in the growth plans for any business. In CPG (consumer packaged goods) it's taken for granted that there will be lots of launches every year to support the brand and build excitement and loyalty across the target consumers. This was not usually the case in specialty chemicals, it's more about how do you make more money with the same chemicals. So the historical focus in Ashland Specialty Ingredients was on line extensions. We began to add more focus on creating new molecules based upon deeper insights into the unmet needs of our customers.

This shift meant more investment and commitment from senior management. In order to successfully secure that support you really need to understand your CEO's stomach for innovation and what they mean by it. As the leader of innovation, you need to be on the same page as the CEO and have a clear agenda that drives in the right direction.

Nancy Shea, VP Global Innovation and Marketing, Ashland

Credible strategy

I have highlighted the need for a clear purpose, ideally a burning platform, combined with an inspirational vision. These can be even more powerful if complemented by a credible strategy. This will bring a number of benefits, as it will provide focus and help with both the internal and external credibility of the programme. It will also inform the decision criteria when prioritising which ideas to focus on, and can help to identify areas of alignment with the core business and hence potential *win-win* partners in the broader business.

Defining this strategy should create a clear understanding of what innovation means for the company and what its role will be. This makes innovation far easier, as it is coherent and becomes almost expected by internal and external stakeholders alike. This is reflected by the Reliant Energy case example below. Reliant Energy's strategy and brand have developed to a point where it now has permission and even an expectation from customers to be innovative and try new things.

Case example: New innovations at Reliant Energy

Reliant's parent company, NRG Energy, is betting big on innovation. Its origins are as a conventional power generator. But in recent years, it has expanded into customer-focused retail and has made huge bets on sustainable and renewable energy, like wind and solar. For our customers, value is created through innovative products and services – simple and seamless – that empower them to have greater control over how they manage their energy usage and their personal energy production.

It includes innovations like smart thermostats, home services and connected home offerings, which are right around the corner for Reliant customers. And with advancements in distributed generation, this will ultimately allow energy consumers to generate much of their own electricity, keeping them connected wherever they are, whatever they are doing, for as long as they are doing it.

It's this type of advancement that sets the bar for others. In fact, we don't see ourselves as just a power company at all. And we certainly couldn't advance with this type of speed and agility if we were an 'old school' utility. NRG is a technology driven service provider organized around the customer.

Scott Burns, Director of Innovation at Reliant, an NRG company

It should be understood that this is not a big corporate strategy exercise. Too much time spent thinking about corporate direction or brand values can lead to warped decision-making and takes focus away from delivering customer-led innovation at pace. Instead, strategy should clarify the thinking behind the burning platform and vision, so that the problem is clearly defined, and hence point towards where to look for the solution. The danger of too much strategy is expressed by Shannon Bryan, GM of Customer Strategy and Planning at Shell:

> "The biggest error is companies being too internally focused and not consumer driven. I often see 'improved' innovations which is just making a current product cheaper or adding some features. Actually, the old one was fine and it's not worth the effort of changing it as consumers aren't dissatisfied with the first one. People aren't really thinking about what problem they're trying to solve, rather just align to some internal strategy."

Shannon Bryan, GM Customer Strategy and Planning, Shell

Once the strategy is clear, goals and objectives can be defined. This may be looking at a revenue number or less commonly, though often more usefully, a market share target. Going back to the underlying burning platform can help inform not just the scale but also the type of objective to be put in place, as evidenced by the TAL case example below.

Case example: Clarifying the strategy at TAL

For pragmatic corporate innovation it needs to be linked to strategy. You know that the organisation has a growth target, and after normal new product development (NPD), corporate development, and efficiencies, there's a gap which is what innovation has to cover. If you know what the revenue gap is each year then it really focuses the mind. But this can still be too blurry so I like to get behind the numbers and understand the value drivers so that focus becomes more around increasing customer retention or accessing new segments.

These then drop into themes, which we make sure are simple and clearly defined. They need to address a combination of strategic, commercial and of course customer issues. It needs to be more than just strategic so that the business is beginning to hurt or at least is worried about the pain so there is more of a burning platform.

The themes are then prioritized. This really helps when people are presenting ideas as they don't need to waste half the time talking about the problem. We've then actually titled these themes around myths. Take content marketing for example, we pay millions of dollars to Google Search and for buying leads as our content hasn't been strong enough to draw people in. If we had compelling content it would be different. We use the quote that 'Life insurance is sold not bought'. We want to break the top ten myths about life insurance so that people can see the importance of innovation and where we have to focus our efforts. We have made a three-minute film about breaking these myths to gain traction around the business.

You almost win or lose straightaway on clarifying the input and the output like this.

Tim Thorne, Chief Innovation & Disruption Officer, TAL

Incentivise the right objectives

Once the purpose is defined, it is important that the corresponding objectives are believable and bold. Clear individual objectives for innovation staff can be hard to set out as so much is unknown, and programmes and their corresponding objectives tend to evolve far quicker than most HR review systems. Additionally, the likely failure rate highlighted below can make this problem more complex still.

For example, it is not uncommon for a business to ask an innovation employee to deliver £x million of new revenue over a certain time period from new innovations. On the surface that may align directly with the business objectives, but in fact this objective is set against a background where the size of the market, the business model, the operational requirements, even the idea itself, is completely unknown. Therefore, it is impossible to know whether such an objective is realistic and it is hardly fair when compared to the objectives for an employee in the core business, where the environment is fully understood.

Clear and realistic objectives are normally possible if broken down in a way that better clarifies the business objectives and aligns them to those of the individual. For example, instead of a broad objective such as to deliver £x million of new revenue, the business should define more specific objectives that will drive the desired growth, such as:

1. Identify key markets with potential and how to win in those markets.

2. Establish an innovation capability to win in these markets.

3. Launch x new propositions (allowing for a failure rate).

4. Demonstrate that the propositions are progressing and evolving quickly based on lessons learned.

5. Demonstrate that the chosen business model(s) maximise market share and profitability.

These objectives align more closely to the real business objectives and if these are successfully delivered they will maximise revenue growth for the business. From an employee's perspective, all of these objectives are now achievable.

Staff incentives are an important part of any objective setting exercise, including innovation programmes. By definition, the corporate environment cannot create the same level of 'skin in the game' for employees as achieved by start-ups, and this will impact everything from recruitment to performance, which makes it even more important to get them right. Ian Price, Director of Sales-mind, put it like this:

> "Somebody taking a salary is not an entrepreneur. If you don't have your mortgage at risk you don't understand."

Ian Price, Director, Sales-Mind

Some firms opt for venture capital-style incentive schemes, which are directly tied to the financial success of new launches. These are rarely valid in a corporate innovation context for a number of reasons:

1. The level of individual risk within a corporation is far lower than with a small start-up, so such a scheme is really only potential upside for an employee. In many situations this will be irrelevant and so it will not impact an employee's performance.

2. The corporate context creates an environment that is far less manageable for the innovation team. The team may have a great idea that could do brilliantly, but for internal reasons the corporation chooses to limit it.

3. Straight financial success may not be aligned with the actual objectives of the corporation, which could be anything from acquiring market share, to reducing overall customer churn, rather than straight profit from a venture. So the wrong behaviours might be incentivised.

4. Placing a team of employees on a potentially far-more rewarding bonus-structure can create additional friction with the rest of the staff. This will not be conducive to cooperation from the staff in the core business.

Therefore, not only is anything more than a standard bonus scheme aligned to the innovation programme's objectives unnecessary, anything more than that may well be detrimental to success. It's important to recognise that this model is far-removed from the risk and reward experienced by entrepreneurs in start-ups.

Given the above challenges in setting objectives, it can be as important to incentivise key behaviours as much as output, although behavioural reviews are notoriously subjective so should only be part of the answer. As always, recognition can be an important tool in driving the right behaviours. Including innovation staff in broader company recognition opportunities – whether at specific events, or an internal newsletter – can help foster an innovative culture, drive the right behaviours and help communicate the innovation message across the broader business. It can also help create permission for trying new approaches and innovations, such as Tata's 'Dare to Try' awards, which recognise promising innovations that failed.

Understand and acknowledge the natural failure rate

Hand in hand with the objectives go a set of implications of what will be required. For example, if the aim is to achieve large new revenue streams in multiple new markets, then the investment required and resources allocated will need to be appropriate. Likewise, implicit in these objectives, there will need to be a clear set of expectations of what success looks like.

For example, research by Stevens and Burley (Research Technology Management Journal, 1997), suggested that on average it takes 3,000 raw ideas to deliver one commercial success, which implies that 2,999 ideas will fail at one stage or another and that much of the associated investment in those 2,999 ideas will also have been lost. Failure is often a dirty word, and whilst many corporates talk about accepting failure in an innovation context, rarely are these words backed by any true understanding of the failure rate or any action to support this.

" It's natural that lots of ideas fall by the wayside,

but these aren't failures

– they are important steps in the process of evolution.

You wouldn't have got the success without the discards.

Failure is discovery. It's just part of the process. **"**

**Paul Wylde, Founder & Creative
Director, PaulWylde**

Perceived project failure remains a massive challenge to corporate innovation programmes. Some of the case examples in this book are anonymous and others were not approved for final inclusion, as companies are still afraid of this perception of failure. Yet despite all of this, if you establish a new programme to enter a range of new products and services into different markets, some of them, many of them even, are destined to fail, even if you're Google. This expectation needs to be understood, managed and supported, both at a corporate level and at the level of the individuals working on the projects. For example, each division of Philips has its own incubator with ten live projects at any given time, on the basis that one of the ten will take off.

a

Case example: Accepting failure as part of success at Google

Google is known for YouTube, not Google Video Player. The thing is, people remember your hits more than your misses. It's okay to fail as long as you learn from your mistakes and correct them fast. Trust me, we've failed plenty of times. Knowing that it's okay to fail can free you up to take risks. And the tech industry is so dynamic that the moment you stop taking risks is the moment you get left behind.

Two of the first projects I worked on at Google, AdSense and Google Answers, were both uncharted territory for the company. While AdSense grew to be a multi-billion-dollar business, Google Answers (which let users post questions and pay an expert for the answer) was retired after four years. We learned a lot in that time, and we were able to apply the knowledge we had gathered to the development of future products. If we'd been afraid to fail, we never would have tried Google Answers or AdSense, and missed an opportunity with each one.

Our growing Google workforce comes to us from all over the world, bringing with them vastly different experiences and backgrounds. A set of strong common principles for a company makes it possible for all its employees to work as one and move forward together. We just need to continue to say 'yes' and resist a culture of 'no', accept the inevitability of failures, and continue iterating until we get things right.

Susan Wojcicki, Google's Senior Vice President of Advertising, in 'The Eight Pillars of Innovation' (Google.com)

Fear of failure by individual employees can be a silent killer of innovation projects. The innovation team may be less radical and challenging to the existing business, and leaders in the core business may withdraw support for the project, even if privately they believe it's a good idea – all because they don't want to be associated with a failed project. So it is important to accept and recognise that a degree of failure is unavoidable.

Many innovation commentators talk of employees needing bravery in the face of this fear of failure, but bravery should not be needed if the appropriate environment exists that permits and even encourages individuals to try new things whilst understanding that not all of them will work.

Having said that, recognising failure needs to be done in such a way that it does not encourage failure. Suitable lessons should be learnt and applied so that failure does not become part of the culture. Indeed, it is not unusual to hear that failure should be accepted without consequence, but this cannot be right. Failure to achieve objectives can mean significant losses or even worse for the business, and a company should not be employing people that regularly fail in their job.

The issue is not with failure per se, but with the implicit mindset and the objectives that are normally set. The best way to approach this is not by setting objectives based around revenue or similar metrics, but by approaching every project and launch as a test. Every test needs to demonstrate that lessons are being learned and applied back into the project or business, so that it is evolving quickly towards success. In this way, staff can be measured and judged on their ability to test hypotheses and quickly learn from them and then act on those lessons. This drives the right behaviours, is measurable, and avoids the challenges of trying to judge performance on the overall outcome of the project, which the staff may have very limited control over. If this happens, then success will soon follow for revenues and other key metrics.

> "In a way there are lots of failures. We try lots of explorations and then present the best to clients and stakeholders. Some get selected, some don't. So it's natural that lots of ideas fall by the wayside, but these aren't failures – they are important steps in the process of evolution. You wouldn't have got the success without the discards. Failure is discovery. It's just part of the process."

Paul Wylde, Founder & Creative Director, PaulWylde

Communicating the role of innovation

Some commentators promote 'stealth' programmes, where innovation can be undertaken outside of the normal office domain, to come up with new opportunities for the company without being bogged down in the usual bureaucracy. Whilst some projects can benefit from gaining momentum before engaging the wider business, if you believe that innovation is important to the future of your company, then it is hard to see why it would be set up as a sideshow and hidden out of sight.

Rather, early, clear and consistent communication of the role of innovation drives internal and external support. Innovation needs to be set up as a core pillar of business strategy and communicated as such so that everybody – and by that I mean everybody from frontline staff to investors to partners to customers – can understand that it's important and why it's important, and then give it the backing it needs to succeed. In practice, this can be immensely difficult, as the message has to be simple enough that people understand it and can repeat it, aspirational enough that people want to repeat it, and credible enough that people actually will repeat it.

This message needs to be consistent and companies can easily trip up if the groundwork has not been done up front. The language of innovation is a common trip hazard. The word *innovation* can mean many different things to different people and clarifying the language is an important first step, though not one that should be laboured over. I have come across more than one organisation who have commenced innovation programmes and spent the first six months or more defining the terminology. That is hardly a strong start for a programme looking to drive speed and minimise bureaucracy. Another common terminology error is simply the name *innovation department*, or when companies try wackier titles like 'id8' or 'Spark'. Such names cause a number of problems right from the start:

∿∿∿> **Vision and scope:** There is an inherent lack of vision, objectives and scope for the new team. Without a clear goal and obvious view of what success looks like, it's very hard for a team just to *innovate*. Even if a clear purpose has been defined, this can be lost sight of over time if not reinforced in communications such as the name.

∿∿∿> **Value:** Without a clear aspiration, it's hard to clearly measure the value of this new department. Investors may like the intention to innovate, but will be unwilling to reflect that in the share price without a stronger link to the broader company strategy or some clear evidence of success. Indeed, such a cloudy investment may even be value destroying.

∿∿∿> **Brand:** The rest of the organisation is likely to resent a new team with a strange name and no clear objectives.

This can be the start of many of the common issues that occur between an innovation team and the rest of the organisation.

Therefore, it pays to think carefully about the name of any new innovation team as well as all communication surrounding the programme, to ensure that it sends a clear message to internal and external stakeholders alike about the focus of the department. It should align with the broader business strategy or, if innovation is at the core of the business, make it the lifeblood of every department in the business.

Terminology and branding is just one aspect of communicating the role of innovation in the organisation. Engaging the core organisation to gain support for individual projects from key executives and functions often requires much time and attention. Understandably, other teams want to feel involved and minimise disruption to their own processes and performance, but equally the innovation team needs to move quickly and not compromise on its objectives.

Communicating early is critical as it enables stakeholders to voice their opinions right at the start and feel like they have been with the process from the beginning. The 'not invented here syndrome', where people in an organisation reject ideas that they have not themselves developed, may be a cliché, but it's all too common and getting input from as many people in the organisation as possible from the outset can play a big role in the success of innovation initiatives. There is no excuse for leaving this to chance, or leaving it so late in the development of the concept that it becomes an easy target for people who are in a position to claim that they have not been consulted.

Case example: Engaging the core organisation to enable innovation at Which?

You have to decide whether you need the core, and if not then it's easiest just to keep away, but often you do. In proposition development at Which?, I always make sure we get everybody involved right from the start. You have to sell it at every level and get their views and challenges and give them the opportunity to contribute. Also, I often make sure I give other directors time to reflect and get comfortable with the new idea. Often, they might dislike it the first time they see something, but once they've come across it in a couple of meetings they get used to the idea and start to see how it might work. You don't necessarily have to change it for them, just don't railroad them. Then you create workshops and so on for the rest of the organisation – get sales and customer service etc. involved and brainstorm out the concepts and let them have their opportunity to input. Then they'll become big backers. It's just good engagement though you still have to have an opinion and drive it through.

Michael Johnson, Former MD New Ventures, Which?

Summary

〰〰⟶ **The purpose of the innovation programme needs to be clearly understood** – Before anything else, it is critical to clearly understand the real reasons for innovation.

〰〰⟶ **Programmes that lack a burning platform, or the fear of a burning platform, have limited chance of success –** Those that lack a sufficiently business critical purpose, or burning platform, will struggle to survive. The strongest case for change includes an aspirational vision as well as an urgent burning platform.

〰〰⟶ **Make sure the level of commitment to innovation and its implications are clearly understood** – On the surface, innovation programmes are sexy and fun, but the reality is long and hard work and distraction from the core business. Be clear on the level of commitment to this reality from the executive leadership team.

◊◊◊◊◊‣ **A credible strategy can make the purpose and vision even more powerful** – This is not about carrying out an exhaustive strategy exercise, but a practical strategy will help credibility, focus and internal alignment, and so improve chances of success.

◊◊◊◊◊‣ **The right objectives can be incentivised and encouraged** – Approaching every project as a test to learn and improve from rather than high level revenue or profit metrics enables a culture of innovation. Personal objectives and incentives are correspondingly easier too.

◊◊◊◊◊‣ **Many fail to properly understand and acknowledge the natural failure rate** – Most innovation projects fail to deliver step-change growth. Corporates often struggle to deal with this failure, or perceived failure, rather than understanding the value of continually improving their offer through the lessons learned.

◊◊◊◊◊‣ **Early, clear and consistent communication of the role of innovation drives internal and external support** – Ensuring alignment with, understanding by and support from employees in the core business is often critical to success, so communication, branding and engaging these employees are some of the most important tasks for corporate innovation teams and executive sponsors.

2. Structure

Choose the structure(s) that match your ambition.

One of the first challenges when establishing innovation in a business is how to structure the team within the organisation and govern their actions. The answer to this question will vary considerably depending on the objectives and type of innovation being implemented.

For example, innovation will be absolutely core to a product-focused consumer electronics company like Samsung or Sony, whilst for traditional service-based companies like utilities, other capabilities such as customer service will be at the heart of the organisation.

Organisational structure can create a number of issues if it's not aligned correctly. Typically, innovation will reflect the structure, so if left in the marketing team you get lots of new marketing campaigns, if in a certain business unit then ideas are constrained to that department – often missing out real customer issues and bigger opportunities as a result, or if simply left too far down the hierarchy then projects will be incremental and fail to gain traction or visibility. With these issues in mind, it's an important consideration.

There are a range of innovation structures that can be established and there is no single set answer as to the best structure. Rather, the role of innovation and the organisational context will define the most suitable structure(s) of the team(s) delivering it.

These structures are not mutually exclusive, so it is not uncommon to find an organisation with a new product development (NPD) team in the core business, a skunk works unit, and a corporate venture capital fund, all supported by a research and development function. Whatever the solution may be, the important thing is to provide clarity of roles and responsibilities to the teams involved.

Understand the purpose upfront

So, there are a range of possible structures for innovation and picking the right one(s) is dependent on the focus of the programme, the company culture, and which function(s) is best placed to deliver it. By far the most important of these is having real clarity over the purpose and vision for innovation.

Case example: Defining the approach before the purpose at the Life & Protection Division of Transamerica

The Transamerica companies are an amalgamation of a number of different organizations, which have been coming together under the Transamerica brand for several years. Even within the Life & Protection Division, there were several operational centres and technology platforms in locations across the US. Bringing everything together required many difficult decisions and changes in day-to-day processes, which in turn affected morale and culture. Divisional leadership decided to meet this challenge head-on by causing additional disruption – this time with innovation. There were two objectives:

1. Positively impact the culture by providing a way for employees to connect and collaborate.

2. Drive growth with a willingness to develop and test products and programs outside the traditional parameters of the business.

It took a while to get any traction, since the focus was on finishing the consolidations. We tried to launch innovation in-house but found it difficult to disrupt ourselves. So we retained outside consultants with specific expertise in helping large organizations establish innovation practices.

The consultants got us going with some good ideas and big black box projects with code names – which that meant nobody could relate to them. After one year, the CEO realized we needed to develop our own innovation expertise so we could customize the approach for our environment.

This started out with a team of three people – two employees and me. The black box projects were wending their way through the development and approvals process so we saw cultural transformation as our top priority. However, three people can't make it happen in an organization of almost 5,000. We had to find an effective and engaging way to reach all our employees and establish channels of communication with all the various areas within the division.

I thought my job was going to be about strategy and insight, but instead, it has been all about people and human behaviour… in other words, coaching, preaching, and demonstrating empathy. It's really tough, trying to change a culture – especially one with roots that in some cases go back over 100 years.

In 2013, we held events in all our locations that started the conversation. The key was listening to employees. We heard that some felt they couldn't innovate as their managers wouldn't let them. Others were concerned that making suggestions about improvements could cost them their jobs. The changes and consolidations had resulted in a significant amount of fear, and when people are afraid, they are less likely to come up with cool ideas. We had a credibility gap and had to demonstrate that ideas and suggestions would be welcomed. We've made considerable progress on this front and there's plenty of opportunity to do more.

Culture is still – and always will be – a critical component but now we are also building the processes and infrastructure to enable change to happen.

Innovation is a journey that for us involves seeding the culture, accessing useful consumer insights, meeting financial targets (including expense management), complying with government regulations and factoring in the intermediaries who help us reach most of our customers.

It's been a process of try, test and learn. It's also required constant adaptation as our organization continues to evolve and new pressures come from external sources. But I'm happy to say that innovation is starting to pop up in unexpected places and the language is becoming part of our vernacular. We're well on our way.

Aaron Proietti, Chief Customer Advocate, Head of Insights & Innovation, Life & Protection Division of Transamerica

Many innovation programmes are set up wrongly as the purpose is not understood upfront. Innovation teams often think they are simply looking for any new growth opportunity in a given market, probably with a focus on larger long-term ideas. However, the most successful teams are always focused around a clear vision and strategy, and will target specific strategic areas, market trends and profit pools. In that way, the programme's purpose can be integrated with the overall business strategy and create harmony, or at least reduce discord, between the programme and the rest of the organisation. In turn this can extend the longevity of the programme and improve the chance of achieving growth of strategic importance.

Incremental innovation

Businesses need to deliver incremental innovation. Keeping the core product portfolio fresh and competitive is fundamental and so most companies will have a team dedicated to this. These teams will be embedded within the core business. Whilst there are myriad alternatives, four structures are most common for innovation teams with a focus on incremental innovation:

1. **New product development (NPD)** – Where companies are typically marketing led and core innovation is focused on new products and services, there is normally an NPD team sitting within the marketing function. Such a team is well positioned to drive new core propositions, supported by strong marketing campaigns integrated with the core business.

2. **Central support** – Central support teams often have a broader scope and act more like internal consultants who support the business by applying innovation approaches, not only to products and services but also to areas beyond classic NPD, covering everything from the customer experience to process efficiencies (as highlighted by the Capital One and Boehringer

Ingelheim examples below). Sometimes, this approach is seen as cheaper than the alternatives as central support teams are typically small, with low funding requirements. However, the reality is that cost is hidden as other business units are resourcing and funding the change, so in reality it is normally just harder to track and manage spend.

3. **Technology-led** – For companies that are more orientated around technology, an R&D team may be tasked with driving innovation. These functions still need to work closely with the core business to ensure that innovation is wanted by customers and is commercially viable for the business.

4. **Temporary** – In some cases, companies identify an opportunity that is slightly different to their standard NPD challenges but which still sits within the core business, such as entering a new category. This creates the opportunity to bring together a focused cross-functional team that is jointly responsible for this one-off project delivery. This structure, with its joint ownership across key business functions, can provide great focus and momentum, but tends to be for more short-term or one-off projects rather than long-term innovation programmes. The case example in Chapter 5 showing the development of Febreze by Procter & Gamble is a great example of this approach.

These four structures are illustrated in Figure 2.1.

Case example: Innovation as a central support function at MetLife

We work with business units to help them unlock innovation potential whether it's new revenues, reduced costs, or a better experience or new ways of working with partners. We're the catalyst that coaches and provides a process. The business has to be committed and provide resource.

Terrance Luciani, VP, Innovation, MetLife

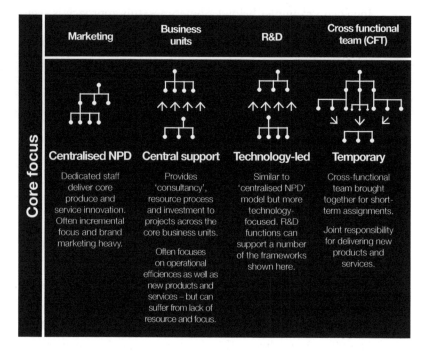

Figure 2.1: Incremental innovation structures

Case example: Applying innovation methodology to transform contact centre experience at Capital One

We had a challenge to make an overseas contact centre great. The performance was good but we wanted to get to great on measures including customer satisfaction, quality and agent satisfaction.

So we got a call to run what we call an innovation GreenHouse programme, to help the team generate and implement some step change ideas.

It was all about getting closer to the work than ever before and pouring in some killer insight to get us thinking differently about the challenge. We interviewed everybody across the different roles to get a 360 view of the work and also sat in India and went through the training and recruitment with the agents. We looked across different industries for inspiration, including Experian, Rolls-Royce, air traffic control and O2. Seeing how others approached achieving excellence really helped us to unlock new thinking and ideas.

The team overhauled and simplified a wide range of processes from hiring and training through to call routing and also redefined what good quality actually means. Ultimately the project helped to cut the error rate in half and raised satisfaction by a third, as well as win an internal award for excellence.

Lee Osborne, Innovation & Digital, Capital One

Case example: Internal Venturing – supporting the core to invest at Boehringer Ingelheim

We run an Internal Venturing programme where we invest in ventures with high returns potential that have often been rejected by the core business. Employees have an idea and really want to do it and they just need a bit of funding or resource to give it a go. The manager might have said no, but once they see that we say yes it feels less risky for them and they typically invest 50% of the funding alongside us or fund the project in full. It's important that they chip in to create ongoing support for the project.

For example, there was a lady in a lab who produces active pharmaceutical ingredients as we need a small amount of active ingredients for testing new products, but this is really expensive as it is customised and only small quantities. She found a new software that predicts the attributes of materials and realised that we could use the software to predict the outcome of the tests rather than produce the active ingredients. The line business was focused on the day job and didn't want to run the trial. So we agreed to invest a few thousand dollars, which the line business then matched, to try it running alongside our normal process and found it to be highly accurate. Now the software is used in our labs across the world and saves us millions of dollars every year, and she is the international project manager, so it's been great for her career too.

Stephan Klaschka, Innovation Director, Boehringer Ingelheim

Case example: Focusing research and development around business needs at Philips

At Philips the broad premise is around design to order – so you have to have a business sponsor and they don't do stuff that's not needed or can't be sold. This works well, particularly where there is a good strategy or category team who are proactive and focused on clear opportunities. The direction is clear and it sounds simple but it's actually really clever. You know the consumer wants it and the retailer can sell it, so you will make money. The opposite is how it used to be with R&D getting a budget and incentivized around getting patents and then trying to push them into the business.

Georgina Schiffers, Former General Manager, Active Play, Philips

Adjacent or step-change innovation

Big businesses need to complement their incremental innovation efforts with adjacent and longer-term innovation to create opportunities for step-change and long-term growth. By definition, teams with this focus need to sit outside of the *business as usual* structure. There are three broad approaches which are commonly found in corporates:

1. **Skunk works** – Create a cross-functional and entrepreneurial team that develops new products and services and ventures in-house. Partners and suppliers may still be used to deliver some elements of the project, but this approach tends to focus on leveraging, building and developing in-house capability. This approaches requires significant nurturing but avoids many of the issues of working with and investing in start-ups.

2. **Accelerator** – This consists of a smaller team to provide a range of benefits such as process, mentoring, support, suitable space, corporate assets and sometimes investment into start-ups. These units can also be focused on internal teams and adopt

a similar approach to the central support approach mentioned above, but with a focus on bigger opportunities and taking the internal teams outside of the core business for a short period, often three to six months.

3. **Corporate venture capital** – This is the least resource-intensive approach and entails establishing a venture capital fund to invest in start-ups in focus areas. This tends to be less hands-on, though corporates will often still provide some mentoring and access to key corporate assets such as sales channels.

These three adjacent structures are summarised in Figure 2.2.

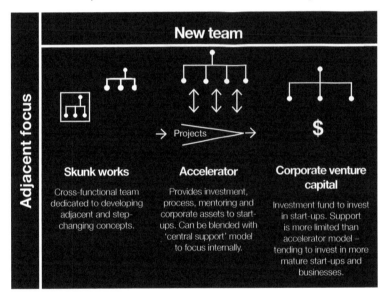

Figure 2.2: Adjacent innovation structures

Holistic structures

Some companies believe that innovation can be achieved by adding it as part of everybody's job description and may even consider that to be an objective in itself. They look to develop a company-wide culture of innovation rather than giving accountability to individual teams. This is seen as a great way to transform the entire culture to be more innovative – it is holistic and everyone is expected to be involved. Figure 2.3 illustrates this structure.

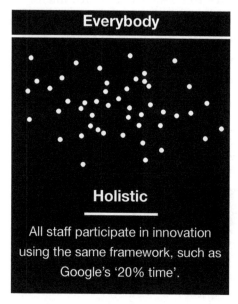

Figure 2.3: Holistic structure

There are a number of instances of this approach working, with perhaps the most famous examples being Google and 3M. Google invests massively in engaging its employees to innovate and has a number of approaches to allow different employees to feed in their ideas. Google cafes are in place to encourage different teams to talk to each other, direct emails to executives are encouraged, and Google Moderator allows employees to vote on key topics they want addressed and questions they want answered at the frequent company-wide meetings. Then, of course, there is the famous '20%' time. By allowing its engineers to spend 20% of their work week on projects that interest them, Google creates strong engagement and has created many of its innovations from this approach, including Google Moderator. 3M is another company which encourages employees to spend time on their own projects and allows 15% of employees' time to be spent *bootlegging*.

Two such successful innovation companies following this policy gives it strong credence, but remember that innovation is the lifeblood for these organisations. This is not the case for many other companies, so it should not be seen as automatically the best thing to do. Also bear in mind that the level of commitment and investment required is substantial. Furthermore, it can lead to small, disjointed projects as there are a large number of part-time supporters rather than focused specialists working on it full-time, and rarely is there sufficient impetus to see these projects through when the teams working on them have their day jobs to focus on.

Sometimes, rather than try to emulate 3M or Google, the objective is as much to improve employee engagement and customer focus as to drive genuine innovation. As a result, the innovation programme is established specifically to engage all employees across the company in innovative ideas, over and above trying to establish the best ideas in the best innovation processes.

These programmes can vary from simple idea suggestion schemes through to larger event-driven programmes with *Dragons' Den* style presentations. The latter tend to be far more successful, but obviously require greater investment. Senior sponsorship is still important, as are high recognition and limited bureaucracy.

However, such programmes must be seen for what they are, which is focused around employee engagement rather than purely innovation. Whilst new innovations often are delivered, the innovations themselves tend to be of an incremental nature and these approaches are rarely the most effective way of establishing strategic innovation in a business. The implication is that they can support long-term cultural change within an organisation, but normally require other innovation structures to deliver more strategic opportunities in the meantime.

Case example: Driving employee engagement at Aviva through an innovation challenge

Aviva is an organisation with a huge passion for the customer experience and in 2008 we decided to launch The Aviva Customer Cup. Each year since then, hundreds of teams have participated in creating bright ideas and bringing them to life to the benefit of Aviva's customers.

The format was simple, we got teams of six people, plus a coach and a sponsor to work on their ideas and compete in the tournament stages, which include a qualifying round, semi-finals and a grand final. The team leader was known as the 'captain' of the project and was often the originator of the idea. Participants came from all levels in the organisation ranging from front-line advisors or engineers to senior executives. Only the highest scoring teams progressed through the tournament until the top ten were selected to attend a prestigious grand final where they presented their ideas to a panel of judges usually made up of a number of executive committee members. Teams finishing in first place in each tournament got to lift the 'cup', an FA cup-sized trophy and this was then engraved with their team name and year of winning.

A huge variety of ideas came to fruition ranging from radical new propositions, or more commonly, innovative process improvements and new ways of working. Every project team was asked to calculate the financial benefits of their project but the main driver was delivering benefits to customers.

For more 'off the wall' ideas, in some iterations of the tournament, teams could apply for seed funding to prototype or demonstrate early benefits of their ideas. The seed funding proved a massive success and enabled projects to move forward more easily.

It worked because it legitimised new ideas. By framing it within a corporately sponsored tournament that was connected to the priorities of the business, innovation became a legitimate way to do business, rather than being seen as a distraction or 'hobby' project. The score sheet included points for being bold and brave to inspire colleagues in breaking through unnecessary bureaucracy and building confidence to work in new ways.

Empowering teams to take responsibility for bringing their ideas to fruition was key in getting approval and funding to continue with future tournaments. By taking ownership of the project, ideas progressed quickly and with greater passion from the team members when compared to traditional ideas schemes where you create an idea then submit it to a panel and is never to be seen again.

At the closure of each tournament, there was always a focus on sharing the benefits across the company. This varied from awarding teams Blue Ribbon certificates on completion of their project, running a benefits realisation tracker, producing animated videos on the top projects, holding Adopt An Idea week and circulating details of how to implement the ideas in other departments. All of these helped, but gaining traction across the company for some of the ideas has been a challenge that still needs more work.

Colleagues who participated found that they could develop new skills in a safe environment, build connections across the company and lead a team (sometimes for the first time). Many colleagues were recognised, promoted and developed as a result of utilising their unrealised strengths. Colleagues from winning teams were also asked to feature in the campaign to promote the next tournament. This included appearing on the front of guidebooks, intranet sites and promotional materials designed for a global audience.

Overall the scheme has been a massive success and a constant source of good news stories as well as driving customer focus and improvements to the bottom line.

Sarah Gregory, Former Head of Customer Innovation, Aviva

Summary

〰〰〜⟩ **Many innovation programmes are set up wrongly as the purpose is not understood upfront** – The important factor is to understand the purpose, culture and intended delivery approach in order to build the right structure(s) from the start.

⤳ **Incremental innovation will generally be delivered by teams embedded in the core business** – There are four common types and choosing the right one is subject to the specific objectives of the programme, company culture and which function(s) is best placed to deliver it.

⤳ **Adjacent or step-change innovation will normally require new teams and structures** – Adjacent innovation teams need to sit outside of the core structure and selecting which of the three common structures is used depends on the intention to lead the delivery of the innovation in-house versus investing in start-ups.

⤳ **Some companies develop a company-wide culture of innovation rather than giving accountability to individual teams** – This works primarily where innovation is at the heart of an organisation, such as at Google, though other organisations often structure employee engagement programmes to drive long-term cultural change towards innovation. These typically drive more incremental opportunities in the short term and require additional focused teams to deliver more strategic innovation.

3. Governance and Leadership

Define a single point of committed ownership.

Clarify the roles and responsibilities across the innovation team and the core business

Corporates launching new products have significant advantages over start-ups trying to do the same thing. Some of these are market facing, such as an established brand or channels to market, but others are in the existing support functions, such as legal, procurement, marketing, research and IT teams.

However, many corporate entrepreneurs complain that these are not advantages at all and in fact are quite the reverse. They suggest that core support functions are geared to support the core business rather than an innovation team and that they are slow, bureaucratic and inflexible. This often leads to an innovation team 'breaking the rules' and either recreating these functions within the innovation team or using external help for these services, which whilst quicker, can also be more expensive and lose much of the knowledge of the core teams. This can obviously also lead to tension and animosity with the core support functions and reduce clarity of employees' roles.

In fact, this is just another classic symptom of poorly established innovation programmes. Innovation teams may complain that the core support functions are not helping, but the real problem

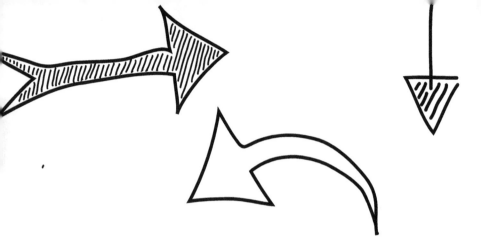

❝❝ Good ideas go off piste when ownership is blurred or confused. ❞❞

Peter Haigh, Director, Energy Market Risk Ltd

is that the governance and structure of the programme are not encouraging them to help. If the senior staff in the support functions are not aware of the importance of the programme and aren't encouraged or incentivised to support it, then of course it's not going to be top of their priority list. The reality is that innovation typically requires many parts of an organisation to work together that are not used to working together. They have their own established processes and are not used to working in this way, creating tension and frustration.

Resolving this issue means first understanding what is central to the innovation programme and the level at which the core business can and should support it. For example, where a requirement of the innovation programme is critical to success, perhaps technology, then the task should be carried out either in-house by the innovation team or in-house by the core IT function, subject to whether the project is also related to the core business systems and the capability of the core IT team. Where a requirement is less critical to the innovation team, perhaps legal support, it can be outsourced to an external supplier – unless the project is closely related to the core business, in which case support from in-house specialists is likely to be more appropriate.

Figure 3.1 shows a decision framework that demonstrates how to select the right approach to leveraging existing knowledge versus building new capabilities, based on the nature of the capability.

Each project is unique, so there is no absolute rule, as some projects may require specialist expertise in branding or IT or patents, whereas others won't. Therefore, companies need to:

〜〜〜> Define a specific relationship between the innovation programme and each of the core functions.

〜〜〜> Make sure that that relationship extends into objective-setting and resource allocation processes.

〜〜〜> Consciously adapt it to work for each individual project.

Implementation: Leverage core capabilities, or, buy, build or partner to acquire new ones?

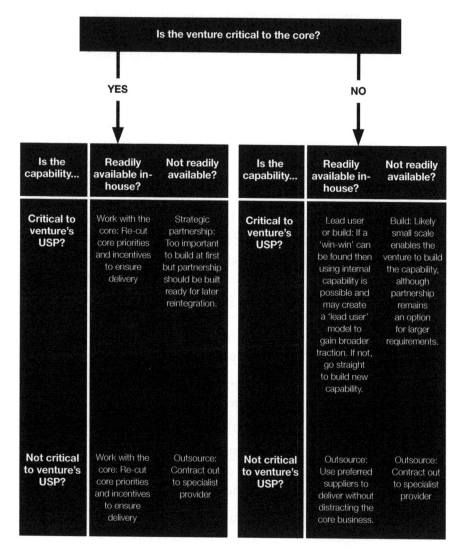

Is the venture critical to the core?					
YES			**NO**		
Is the capability...	**Readily available in-house?**	**Not readily available?**	**Is the capability...**	**Readily available in-house?**	**Not readily available?**
Critical to venture's USP?	Work with the core: Re-cut core priorities and incentives to ensure delivery	Strategic partnership: Too important to build at first but partnership should be built ready for later reintegration.	**Critical to venture's USP?**	Lead user or build: If a 'win-win' can be found then using internal capability is possible and may create a 'lead user' model to gain broader traction. If not, go straight to build new capability.	Build: Likely small scale enables the venture to build the capability, although partnership remains an option for larger requirements.
Not critical to venture's USP?	Work with the core: Re-cut core priorities and incentives to ensure delivery	Outsource: Contract out to specialist provider	**Not critical to venture's USP?**	Outsource: Use preferred suppliers to deliver without distracting the core business.	Outsource: Contract out to specialist provider

Figure 3.1: Defining roles for implementation

Getting these things right can mean fundamentally leveraging some of the advantages that the big business has over start-ups, whereas getting it wrong can lead to confusion, delay, resentment and additional cost. More than once, I have witnessed companies with multiple projects addressing the same growth opportunity, in some cases with different consultancies working to the identical briefs, simply because of a lack of clarity and communication of roles and responsibilities in the business.

Case example: Setting up in competition with yourself at Meridian

Powershop is a retail energy company and an independent, wholly owned subsidiary of one of the largest generators in New Zealand. Powershop was conceived as a challenger to traditional electricity offerings, putting customers first by providing an entirely online service that gives users insight into the amount of electricity they consume and how much it will cost before billing them. Powershop customers don't just pay for power, they buy it knowing how much they need like a consumer good.

The principal founder and CEO, Ari Sargent, saw that the last stage in deregulation of the industry was the empowerment of customers. This drove the vision for Powershop to enable real customer engagement in the power they use. Co-founder, Simon Coley, led the design of Powershop's brand development and customer experience. "We saw an opportunity to differentiate the experience for electricity customers that just wasn't happening. Before we launched Powershop most people saw the only difference between power companies was the colour of the bill.

We had to distance ourselves from traditional electricity companies' service offerings, hence the new brand. We kept quiet about Meridian at the start because we were worried that would confuse people. Paradoxically, to innovate in a market as complex and resource hungry as energy we still needed the knowledge, access to infrastructure and the backing of a parent with a significant stake in the market; Meridian.

We developed Powershop independently of Meridian Energy setting up as a kind of skunk works reporting direct to the CEO. Having supportive ownership and only needing to show progress to a few key people made a huge difference to our development. We were given a lot of freedom to experiment but we still needed somebody walking the halls of our parent company. It helped to know the machinations of the corporate environment. Ideas like Powershop are pretty fragile in their infancy and can die if they don't get the air cover they need. The first thing we did was move out of the headquarters and down the road. The more progress we made, the less we saw of them.

When we started poaching their customers things began to change, but that's inevitable. From a group perspective we ended up in competition with ourselves, but it was healthy competition as we've ultimately grown the groups' share of the market and what we've learnt about customer experience appears to have improved both parties. At first we weren't entirely liked by the retail team at Meridian but the board liked our progress, particularly once we began making money."

Simon Coley, Design and Creative Director, Powershop

Once the structure is understood and the roles clarified, attention can turn to how to successfully govern the innovation programme; tie it closely to the core and it can quickly become bogged down in bureaucracy, but letting it run free can increase the risk and miss out on leveraging some of the assets of the business.

Governance can be a particular challenge for those adjacent and longer-term programmes which sit in a standalone unit. Here, rather than working within the standard business parameters and processes, the mandate often involves challenging the status quo, which can create massive friction with other parts of the business. So, how should a standalone innovation unit be managed?

A single point of executive board level sponsorship

Many innovation units have unsuitable governance. Often, core innovation teams are hidden under a broader division such as marketing or strategy, where they can suffer from a lack of focus and executive sponsorship. Likewise, establishing a new

ff You can't innovate by committee 55

standalone innovation unit often results in the creation of some sort of steering committee where executives from across the core business, together with the innovation leader, meet regularly to make decisions on the ideas and projects in the pipeline.

Innovation committees may sound sensible as a way of achieving buy-in from key stakeholders and giving a rounded view to the decision-making process. Indeed, there are a number of benefits to it, as it forces the innovation team to engage the core business and look for ways of leveraging core assets and minimising disruption to the core. However, in practice such committees tend to slow down projects. Normally, some business units or individuals will be against the idea, whilst others might want it for themselves. Some will not be interested and too busy with their own challenges to support it, and others will be too risk-averse to give the right direction, plus such a steering group typically results in more questions being asked than decisions taken. Most managers in an organisation are targeted and incentivised on optimising their operations, which means they want an unchanging environment that they can tweak and polish to maximise efficiencies. The last thing they want is change, exceptions to the rule, or added complexity. You can't innovate by committee.

An innovation programme will always have enemies as by definition it is seeking to change the established order, and there is a high chance that some of these enemies will sit on a given steering group. In this way, it becomes the perfect forum for delay as it gives a level of power and control to these core business leaders who have comparatively little to gain – or even much to lose – from driving an innovation programme to succeed.

So a steering committee alone rarely leads to fast innovation, but with C-suite involvement this can be changed. If the projects are truly important, an executive sponsor from the board of the business or business division should be tasked with driving them forward and empowered to do so. If not prepared to do this, then it may be time to question the importance of the purpose and burning platform described in chapter 1. If it is not important, then the company should not be investing in it in the first place.

Case example: CEO sponsorship driving successful innovation at Barclays

When we built a new bank for Barclays in Germany, everyone was aware that the CEO had effectively already made the decision to do it and so they were therefore focused on how to make it work rather than a do we/ don't we conversation. This gave massive momentum to the project which ended up wildly beating its targets.

Phil Clarke, Partner, Market Gravity

Without such senior support and involvement in the governance, an innovation team can only become bogged down in the usual politics and will inevitably lose focus and support as other areas of the business become the centre of attention for targets and budgets. The CEO and board should be heavily engaged if the original purpose of the innovation programme has been correctly established, i.e. it is in line with the overall corporate strategy, as shown in the Powershop example above. When the innovation programme is an important part of corporate strategy, then the board will be fully engaged in the steering and output of the programme, and decision-making will be speeded up considerably.

With this level of backing, other business unit leaders will typically be more inclined to support an innovation programme, or at least hinder it less, rather than steering the programme towards their own benefit. Getting such buy-in from the senior board may seem challenging and ambitious, but it is the only way to establish a really successful innovation programme. The likes of Jeff Bezos and Bill Gates are testament to what happens when CEOs and boards drive innovation from the top.

It can still be important to create a forum to keep other stakeholders on board and up to date. Sceptical colleagues will find ways to undermine an innovation project. However, keeping them close to the project and aware of its importance and momentum, as well as identifying benefits for them, can help minimise disruption from this group.

Case example: Frustrating governance at Kodak

We were 20 people carved off with direct reporting to the CMO and access to the CEO so we should have had the sponsorship to do well. We had some good ideas and one in particular was a concept very similar to Instagram that instead digitized the visual qualities of Kodak's film – we had a great business plan, and working prototype and Kodak had the brand to do it well.

We had really good insights and a good multidisciplinary team. However, once it came down to execution, an advisory council was formed comprised of the heads of all the business groups. Companies often create advisory councils like this and get too many people involved and too many agendas. The existing business and bonuses are geared towards short-term horizons and the current business model, so they'll end up undermining the project even if they don't realise they are doing it.

In this case, they had a monopoly on all their own businesses. Kodak then was incredibly vertically integrated – they didn't just own the manufacturing plant but also the farms producing the raw materials like gelatines that went into the factories. This meant that the core had massive profitability and a very strong culture around protecting this. It created unrealistic expectations on any new innovation. No innovation could get to that level of vertical integration and profitability so it was just killed. They needed to work out a way of eating themselves but couldn't.

Tom Hobbs, Former Creative Director, UI Design Strategy, Eastman Kodak

---

The level of commitment and focus by the owner and sponsor will determine success

C-Suite support is not necessarily enough, or rather, it depends what is meant by support. In some cases, *support* can be passive or confined to verbal support, when what we really mean by support is proactive engagement that is committed to addressing the purpose of the innovation programme. Even when the CEO is supportive, such as in the Kodak example, without proactive engagement it may not be enough to overcome the barriers within the core business and ensure success. So the owner and leader of the programme need to be fully committed to, and focused on, the programme. This means performance metrics, objectives and incentives need to be aligned, and sufficient time created to enable focus on it.

Case example: CEO action driving strategic change at Marks & Spencer

In 2007, Marks & Spencer (M&S), a leading UK retailer, launched a five-year, £200 million sustainability programme, Plan A, which has since transformed many of its operations around sustainable business principles. This was strategic innovation. Not a new product, but transformational innovation and the programme had the ingredients for success:

- A capable business looking to the future and seeing the need for change.

- A CEO with a vision and belief in the need for change.

- A talented team with a clear brief to get a plan to deliver that vision.

- A strong cause – based on a theme that would resonate with M&S customers and colleagues.

Nevertheless there were a lot of challenges right from the start. Despite the talented people behind Plan A there were inevitably people wondering what the CEO was on about. They were busy focusing on profitably serving customers in a tough retail world and didn't see sustainability as a commercial priority. So there was lots of resistance before the idea was developed and launched. Critical to overcoming this were the sponsorship by the CEO and the senior people who got involved early on:

- The exec director given responsibility for Plan A became a massive advocate after an epiphany moment during some experiential research when he met with an 'eco warrior'. She was passionate about sustainability, well informed and un-hypocritical in her actions. He realized that he had to become similarly well informed, and as a result, passionate too and perhaps most importantly by connecting what he did in the business to those same principles he could make a difference at scale.

- An external big hitter was given 'carte blanche' by the CEO to go around the organization and speak to anybody to get a real view of Plan A's progress. This provided the CEO with a clear and independent perspective on how it was going. He was very blunt with no axe to grind and the CEO became well informed.

However, it's an error to think that because the boss is on board that everybody would get involved or that even great ideas will happen without a lot of help. Some of the business line heads just weren't that interested, but the CEO did some interesting things to overcome that:

- He promoted key resistors onto key roles in the Plan A working groups. At first I thought this was bad news but before long they were standing up at conferences shouting about all of Plan A's achievements. This forced an 'honesty' into how the plan was delivered – they knew they had a long way to go, lots to change, but that the right people would be fully committed to doing it.

- He changed the language from CSR to 'How we do business' even threatening to fire key people if they were still talking about CSR at the launch. This was not some side initiative for the annual report, but about the whole business. Before you knew it, the CSR committee became the 'How we do Business committee' run by the business lines.

On all innovation projects, people chip away at the idea and it becomes the same old rubbish with some extra polish on. There is so much compromise that it's rare to find something that stays true to the vision, but I'm fortunate enough to have worked with the Plan A team and it's still working.

Simon Brown, Managing Director, ADEC Innovations

Summary

〰〰〰⟶ **Clarify the roles and responsibilities across the innovation team and the core business** – Many companies fail to define a clear business owner and the right working relationship, if any, with the core business and support functions, leading to corporate *treacle*.

〰〰〰⟶ **Innovation units require a single point of executive board level sponsorship** – Steering groups are inappropriate if given a decision-making mandate. Stakeholders do need engaging but decision-making needs a direct line to a single owner at the top.

〰〰〰⟶ **The level of commitment and focus by the owner and sponsor will determine success** – Handing an innovation challenge to a talented leader to deliver on top of their day job is not a recipe for success. It needs focus (i.e. time available) and a level of commitment (i.e. incentives and objectives aligned), and an equally committed sponsor to smooth the path.

4. Methodology and Process

Select the right approach for the context and objectives.

There are countless frameworks, approaches and methodologies to deliver innovation programmes and projects and choosing the right one for your situation can have a big impact on the programme's success. Questions such as should the programme be *open* or *closed*, or should it follow agile and lean start-up principles, are common.

Currently, there is a trend towards open innovation and agile methodologies. Too many companies are happy to follow these fashionable approaches without understanding whether or not it is appropriate for their situation or how best to deploy them. Innovation leaders should be designing the methodology that best suits the programme's objectives and the business context, rather than automatically choosing *open* over *closed*, and *agile* over the classic *waterfall model*, in which the design process is carried out as an integrated, sequential process to build the whole solution from a master plan.

Open innovation

There is currently a lot of corporate activity in *open innovation*, which means including external parties such as customers, suppliers and partners in the innovation process. Many companies have moved in this direction, such as Unilever, Tesco, Procter & Gamble, Philips and Lego, and it can bring some obvious benefits.

For example, GE has partnered with Quirky to deliver a crowd-sourced innovation platform through which a community identifies and prioritises product ideas based on GE patents, which are then developed, manufactured and distributed through stores like Best Buy and Target. The first products include a smart air conditioner, a connected home dashboard and an internet-connected power strip, all connected through GE's smart-home platform.

There are some obvious areas where open innovation is particularly beneficial, such as:

〰〰〰> **When entering a market outside of the core business** – Following an open innovation methodology and including suppliers and partners from that industry can bring market expertise to the project far more rapidly than following a closed route.

〰〰〰> **As projects approach implementation phase** – Open innovation can bring broader expertise to deliver a more robust solution than going it alone, and often more quickly too.

Involving customers throughout the innovation process, though not without its dangers, is almost always a value-adding exercise (which I'll discuss further in chapters 6 and 7), but the inclusion of other companies in the process does come with some clear caveats. When establishing innovation, I have highlighted the importance of a clear purpose, vision, strong governance and an innovative culture. All of these fundamentals are undermined when working with a third party, as the purpose, vision and roadmaps normally differ, co-location is unlikely and culture is rarely the same.

Further, while opening up a project early can bring great benefits, equally it may be done before the proposition is finalised and hence the open partners could turn out to be wrong for that project, or even be competitors to the final offering. Likewise, the process and objectives need to be clear and transparent to all parties involved from the beginning to avoid misaligned expectations and additional bureaucracy. So open innovation is not a silver bullet.

That said, there are instances where it works well and the Orange example below shows how digital projects in particular can be ideal for open innovation, if done in the right way.

Case example: Leveraging the digital world for open innovation at Orange

Often we look forward for co-creation and cooperation with external partners in an open innovation approach. Orange has developed a comprehensive range of open innovation actions at international scale: Orange Fab (start-up accelerator), Orange Partner (application programming interface (API) exposure), Orange 4 Development (incubators network), Imagine with Orange (innovation crowdsourcing).

Various problems can occur: one has to cross borders such as cultural gaps, a lack of trust, building a shared vision, mobilizing dedicated resources for co-innovation, tweaking vertical organization for transversal cooperation, developing knowledge sharing and networking. Partners often have their own priorities and roadmaps. So open innovation means alignment which is not always natural. It requires a lot of flexibility.

However, in the digital world we can rely on APIs that can let partners work together more effectively. Moreover digital has become paramount, a common layer for innovation, and it is all the more true with the Internet of Things, linking every object and turning many domains into Smart domains: Smart Phones, Smart Homes, Smart Cars, Smart Retail, and Smart Cities.

Three years ago we built a platform that could feed our TV service on TV, tablet and phone with social conversations filtered from Twitter (Social TV). Because of the API structure, various Orange applications were able to use the platform and capture the buzz not only around TV shows but on sports events or video games.

We were able to connect quickly and simultaneously with several partners and other business units at Orange through the API. It's far easier and more flexible as it has explicit knowledge and functionality in the instructions. Because of this clarity and simplicity, it was easy to attract partners, build a community of users, and drive growth of the platform. API also enables us to decouple innovation work streams: we were working on the API evolutions, while API customers were creating value on top of it, without interfering. API automatically creates parameters that side-line many of the normal issues associated with working with partners on open innovation. I was happy to repeat this successful experience initiating an API Toolbox for African mobile entrepreneurs, presenting a whole range of Orange APIs.

Nicolas Bry, Senior VP Innovation, Orange Vallée

Lean methodology

Another methodology that is currently gaining much traction to help improve both the speed and quality of innovation programmes is *lean* or *agile* start-up methodology, which was developed as a way of reducing unnecessary time and cost when developing new products and services.

Conventional wisdom has dictated that companies should fully investigate the viability of new projects before signing off investments in them. This means that processes and experiences are designed, strategies are planned, financial cases are invented, risks are identified and mitigated, and customer research is carried out, and so on. This is all managed through a series of stage-gates where individual ideas have to meet certain criteria at each decision point to progress to the next stage of development and the next level of detail. Only once all the questions are answered is the project piloted and launched. It is understandable how this process has evolved, after all corporates have to manage their investments and brands in line with the expectations of shareholders and demonstrate that they are in control. However,

❝ Lean should be viewed as a mindset, an ethos, **that seeks to minimise waste and** maximise speed. **With those tenets as a guide,** lean can be applied to any industry. **❞**

this process is slow and cumbersome – the opposite traits to those desired in innovation.

In contrast, the lean start-up premise is based around developing a minimum viable proposition (MVP) quickly, testing it with live customers and then iterating the proposition based on their feedback through a series of releases along the lines of the traditional stage-gate process. In this way, business cases, operating plans and so on are not even considered until after the project has demonstrated real potential with customers, and if it fails, it will have failed fast and cheaply. This reduces risk and wasted effort, but again comes with caveats. Culturally, trying to shift from stage-gate to lean, from waterfall to agile, is a massive change in approach and is a huge challenge. Lean can still fall foul of many of the normal innovation challenges highlighted in this book.

Lean methodology is not something that can be embraced half-heartedly, it needs to be properly understood and implemented to be successful. To go lean means not just to put in place a lean methodology for the innovation team, but also for them to be able to ignore many other processes in the business. In the traditional model, projects will not only follow the classic stage-gate process of the innovation team, but also the various other processes within the company depending on how standalone the unit is. Often other departments will have their own approved suppliers, own processes, and own priorities, and an innovation project will have to navigate these just like any other internal project, be it to acquire marketing budget, or procurement sign-off.

However, none of this is compatible with a lean methodology, which by definition has to be a totally standalone unit, unless the entire organisation operates on lean principles. So the question of whether to shift to a lean methodology becomes subservient to the structure question which has been addressed above, and depends on the purpose of the innovation programme and the proximity of the project to the core.

One challenge I often hear is that the lean start-up methodology "can't work in my industry." There are still those industries where traditional processes are seen as king: for example, pharmaceuticals requires extensive drug testing and clinical trial approvals, and financial services requires highly secure and reliable transactions, so they surely can't employ lean methodologies? It is true that lean methodology evolved in a digital environment where changing a website and testing it can be done overnight, but it is now being applied successfully in many other industries, including those listed above.

In fact, lean should be viewed as a mindset, as an ethos, that seeks to minimise waste, reduce risk and maximise speed in a commercial proposition. The process itself may vary, but with those tenets as a guide, lean can be applied to any industry – even in the B2B healthcare industry, as shown in the Xerox case example.

The words *minimum viable proposition* were chosen carefully. The meaning of *minimum viable* can vary significantly depending on the product and the industry. So, going back to our banking example, minimum will still require strong security and reliability as customers will not touch it if it does not meet normal banking standards. However, minimum may mean that many non-core features can be ignored in the first iteration. MVP means it needs to be good enough for customers to still buy in to the proposition and use it.

Case example: Adapting the agile approach to the healthcare industry at Xerox

Applying agile depends on what you're working on and the business sector you are in. In Healthcare within the US, we are heavily regulated and have

FDA approval for certain solutions. What we've done is explored some of the highly regulated research offshore through incubation and partner. We did this with healthcare sensing and applied the same approach for our crowdsourcing pilot. This is an important option since the pace at which healthcare solutions are being introduced is so fast. It's faster and cheaper to test healthcare solutions subject to FDA approval or regulations offshore, get it right, and then get FDA approval and bring it onshore.

Even then, the hardest thing is getting the pilot off the ground with a customer. The customer is taking a big risk with you on an untested solution, which may or may not work out. It takes time to cultivate that level of trust with a customer and get the green light to pilot. By the time you've accomplished this, signed NDAs and run the pilot, it can take a year and innovation teams just don't allow enough lag time in their plans for all of that to happen.

Agile is great, but you have to have a customer aligned for business to business projects, otherwise it's just an idea that you are working on.

Denise Fletcher, Chief Innovation Officer, Healthcare & Pharma, Xerox

---

A platform approach enables both open and lean methodologies

Similar to enabling a more open approach as in the Orange API example above, a platform-led approach can also enable a more agile approach. Creating a single platform that all the products sit on means that to add new products and propositions can be relatively far quicker as many of the core platform elements are already built and focus can be dedicated to the specific proposition. This can save building many of the core systems such as billing, customer relationship management (CRM) or account management every time that a new product is being developed.

Case example: Lean methodology driving faster commercialisation of innovation at Thomson Reuters

a

We focused on the platform, which in itself was a shift as traditionally Thomson Reuters had been a product company. A few years ago we decided to create an access point for customers to all of our products (as we'd grown by acquisition they were all separate). So we built a single shared infrastructure platform that brought them all together. We took the capabilities from the legacy systems and recreated them on the new platform. This way you do the grunt work of building the platform once, and then you can focus on the exciting stuff. Now we can rollout capabilities very quickly and commercialise them straightaway.

Lean and open are really just two aspects of facilitating innovation. To do innovation well you've just got to try out lots of ideas. There's no other way around it. Innovation is not about waking up in the night with brilliant ideas. You just have to keep trying and tweaking and you eventually hit upon something. 99% of stuff is thrown away. Innovation is small. To afford it, trials have to be quick and cheap. If not, then don't do it. The lower the cost, the more you can do.

You have to work out how to do things cheap and easily. You have to ask what does doing the absolute minimum look like in each case. The platform enables this in our case as it gives us the leverage to be lean. Lean is all about risk management and it also has the upside that it means we can commercialize opportunities far more quickly.

Philip Brittan, Chief Technology Officer, Thomson Reuters

Finally, there is one overriding caveat to all of these methodologies. All of them are designed to bring order and systematic method to innovation. All of them have their merits if deployed correctly, and it is important to employ practical process, but choosing one process or framework over another does not matter if the other factors such as governance and purpose are not properly considered when establishing an innovation programme.

Stage-gate process plays a key role

Corporate entrepreneurs are radical thinkers by definition. They tend to focus on delivering a new proposition above all else, and often view process as one of the barriers in their way. The stage-gate process is a great example and there is an increasingly common belief that stage-gate processes don't work. The challenge is that in the 50 years or so since they were first developed, conversion rates of ideas into successful launches have maintained steady at a very low level and that in fact organisations that use stage-gate processes are no more effective than organisations which have no process at all (Stevens and Burley, 2003).

What this challenge does not account for is the way a stage-gate process is managed. When established in the common way with a cross-functional steering committee and limited sponsorship

ᵃᵃ It's important for a corporate to have governance – that's the difference from a start-up. ᵃᵃ

Phil Kohler, Proposition Director,
British Gas

from above, it is easy to see why a stage-gate process will struggle to be effective, as would any process. However, with CEO or board-level leadership many of the issues of protecting turf, resistance to process change or avoiding additional cost for one of the core areas can be nullified.

It's also important to understand the role that stage-gate processes play. In addition to reviewing the portfolio to make sure the best ideas are getting the right level of focus and that the bad ideas are being killed, they are also about managing risk. Unlike start-ups, large corporates typically have significant assets, such as their brand, that may be impacted by a misguided innovation launch. Therefore, the role of the stage-gate process is also to ensure risks around the innovation programme are understood and managed.

Case example: Stage-gate process at British Gas

Despite some of the difficulties with it, I have a steering group process which you have to have for regulatory and risk management. You are spending a lot of money and need to dot the I's and cross the T's. It's important for a corporate to have governance – that's the difference from a start-up!

Phil Kohler, Proposition Director, British Gas

Traditionally, most stage-gate processes are set as a default barrier. This means that unless projects prove certain things then they do not progress. An alternative to this that some companies have started using is to default to a positive outcome, whereby projects automatically proceed through the stage-gate unless stopped for specific reasons. This creates a natural momentum for projects and reduces the risk of stage-gates unnecessarily slowing down projects, but it needs to be right for the individual company context.

Therefore, just because process exists, it does not mean that it has to be slow, bureaucratic and inflexible. If the process is aligned to the objectives and governed in the right way, then the process should be about helping the innovation team focus on the right areas and improve their proposition as well as managing risk – all in a timely way.

Summary

〰〰〰⟩ **Open innovation is not a silver bullet, but can add great value in certain situations** – Open innovation methodologies can bring great benefits, especially in the digital environment, but have many caveats around when and how to deploy them successfully.

〰〰〰⟩ **Lean methodology can bring many benefits, but is a massive shift in approach and needs to be properly understood and implemented to be successful** – The lean start-up ethos is binary and needs to be embraced fully to work. When it does, it can reduce risk, cost and improve time to market in almost any company in any industry.

〰〰〰⟩ **A platform approach enables both open and lean methodologies** – Create a single platform so that the core platform elements such as billing and CRM are already built and consistent, and focus can be dedicated to rapidly building the specific propositions.

〰〰〰⟩ **Process plays a key role, despite fears of bureaucracy and inflexibility** – Unlike start-ups, big businesses have to protect their brand and shareholders' investment, so process plays a key role in managing risk and should not be abandoned or ignored. If established in the right way with regards to sponsorship and governance then stage-gate processes need not be slow, bureaucratic or inflexible.

5. People, Skills and Culture

Empower a dedicated, diverse and co-located cross-functional team.

Many firms put a lot of focus on the right structure and governance for their innovation programme, but it is the right people and culture that represent one of the keys to success. The research interviews for this book consistently highlighted this as one of the most important aspects of innovation.

A dedicated and specialist team operating in the right culture

As we know, corporate innovation is hard, and trying to attempt it on a part-time or amateur basis normally results in failure. Successful innovation is fast-paced, flexible and resilient and therefore teams working on it need to be fully focused on it, empowered to get on with it, and able to dedicate both their minds and their daily activities to it. Just like other functions such as finance, HR or procurement, employees across the company need to be aware of the right behaviours and processes for innovation, but it should be a dedicated professional team that is focused on delivering it.

Further, it's not just the focus of the team but also its composition that is important. A particular set of attributes are required for successful innovation inside large corporates and even when

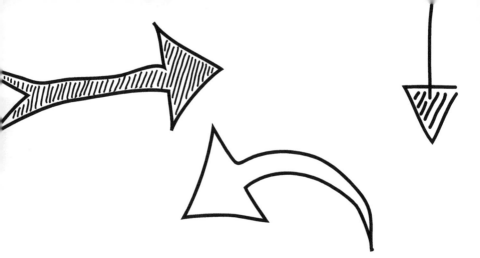

" People make the difference,
not the process.
If genuinely inquisitive, then they will
read between the lines and find nuggets. "

**Meldrum Duncan, Co-Founder,
Curious Industry**

companies put their best people on it or recruit external talent, they're not always putting the right people into the role. A great example of focusing on the right people is at Coca-Cola, which has taken this idea to heart with the Coca-Cola Founders programme. The programme recruits proven entrepreneurs and focuses them on business challenges. This belief in the importance of getting the right people to address their innovation challenges has already resulted in a number of successes, such as the impressive Wonolo.

Broadly, successful intrapreneurs need a few specific attributes, such as perseverance and resilience to keep on fighting for ideas when they are knocked back, willingness to take risks, optimism that ideas can work, creativity to invent and improve ideas, passion for the vision, curiosity to identify and solve problems, and diplomacy around a wide set of stakeholders. These attributes may be found anywhere in an organisation, not just on the management fast-track programme, nor are these attributes exactly the same as those required for entrepreneurship in a start-up sense, where the challenges of navigating a large business are alien.

It is common to hear commentators talk about the right types of people for innovation, yet a number of these *classic* traits are in fact far from reality. For example, fear is seen as a barrier so people should be brave; innovation is all about breaking the rules so mavericks are ideal; taking risks is a good thing to give innovation a chance. In reality, none of this is true, and in the right context then the opposite is often true. For instance, if the processes are adapted to facilitate innovation then the rules don't need to be broken and in fact should be explicitly followed as they are deliberately there to manage successful innovation and minimise corporate risk.

Culture will play a big part of this and only in the right culture will intrapreneurial individuals thrive. Culture can be bottom up, but generally comes from the top. The behaviour of the top executive

CULTURAL VALUES	INDIVIDUAL ATTRIBUTES
Let people do their jobs	**Responsible**
This requires strong role clarity and autonomy so individuals know who is responsible for what, combined with mutual trust and respect to let people actually do it and try new ways of doing it. At the same time those individuals are accountable for the delivery.	Natural willingness to take responsibility for delivery and for their own actions. Also need to combine networking skills to maximise the right support around the organisation with a willingness to be open to sharing their viewpoints – they have to be able to openly voice concerns if they are to be responsible for something.
Expect people to stick to the rules	**Disciplined**
Often 'breaking the rules' is touted as a sign of a good entrepreneur. The reality is that it's simply a sign that the processes aren't right and the company isn't letting people do their jobs (see above). I cannot think of a reason why that is a good thing. Rather, the rules and processes should be practical and efficient so that there is no need to break them. Too often, corporates try to apply the standard organisational rules and processes to innovation, when a more practical approach is required.	A tendency towards discipline and following process correctly can optimise chances of success – if the process are practical and appropriate.
Avoid unnecessary risks	**Prudent (not brave)**
It is common to hear about corporate entrepreneurs taking risks as if it's a good thing. Whilst the culture should be open to new ideas that challenge the status quo, the culture should be risk averse as this can in fact help maximise the chances of successful innovation by not taking unnecessarily high risks or risks that aren't mitigated as much as they could be.	A commonly held view is that corporate entrepreneurs need to be brave. If the culture and environment is right then this should not be true, rather individuals should have a balanced view towards risk with a desire to mitigate it. Risk takers may well have a high tendency to launch new businesses, but this does not necessarily correlate with the success of those businesses.
Establish a strategic vision	**Committed and focused**
Make sure that people are inspired and focused on doing the right things rather than just doing things right.	Belief in the vision and the team around them can drive the dedication, care and perseverance that is required for success. It will also help ensure they stay focused on the key tasks despite many other avenues calling for their attention.
Action-orientated	**Energetic**
Some corporate cultures can tend towards 'analysis-paralysis' where issues and projects are over-analysed with a reluctance to take action. Innovation thrives when there is a sense of urgency and a 'let's just go try it' mindset.	Have the drive and energy to roll up their sleeves and take proactive action.
Challenge	**Creative and curious, with resilient optimism**
Just as the organisational beliefs and assumptions, the status quo, should be challenged by the innovators, so should their ideas and projects be constructively challenged with high expectations of what good looks like.	Always observing and listening and then asking why things are like they are and looking for new solutions can help identify many opportunities. This needs to go hand-in-hand with a tenacious optimism to enable them to persevere in a challenging environment. No ideas will ever move forward if there is not a natural belief that it might work.
Recognition and reward	**Ambitious**
An innovation team can be a tough and lonely role so it is even more important to ensure that success is recognised and rewarded regularly and appropriately.	Innovators are often naturally ambitious to improve, develop and succeed and this is an important characteristic in their ability to have high standards (they are often overly perfectionist if anything) and go the extra mile to achieve them.

Table 5.1. Culture and team

team normally ripples right down to every employee and will define a company's culture. For an innovation programme to have the best chances of success, this culture needs a range of qualities which go hand in hand with the most appropriate individual attributes of the team, as set out in Table 5.1.

Table 5.1 highlights a wide range of personal attributes and not all of the team will possess all of these attributes, but successful teams will benefit from as many of these behaviours and attributes as possible. Where teams and individuals do possess these attributes, and work in a culture close to the one described in the table, then there will be a natural sense of fun and enjoyment. This is a sign that the culture is working and that the people are appropriate. One of the ways of keeping the optimism and resilience of the team alive and well is to ensure a sense of enjoyment, and the creativity, flexibility and openness to push new boundaries can all be fostered by keeping a buzz in the team culture.

"The key is that innovation is fun. If it's not fun for you, then don't engage. It's hard so if not fun it's even more difficult to succeed. You need to rely on the right team with a common vision of what they are trying to achieve. An expert team is key to the fun, with specialists in fields of coding or UI or marketing or pricing all working collaboratively, being able to communicate with each other, aligned like a rugby team, streamlining knowledge circulation."

Nicolas Bry, Senior VP Innovation, Orange Vallée

A dedicated team also means a consistent one. For example, handing over projects from an *ideas* team to an *implementation* team loses momentum, understanding and, most importantly, passion. Innovation is driven by passionate people. If it is divided into chunks with handovers it normally fails, because somebody along the way doesn't have the passion. You have to have one passionate champion to own it from start to finish.

Small cross-functional teams

It is rare to meet somebody who heads up an innovation team who doesn't claim to be under-resourced, and yet the most successful teams are often small ones. Large teams can become unwieldy and begin to lose the ability to make fast decisions and adapt quickly. Large teams suddenly need to spend time bringing each other up to speed and gaining buy-in amongst themselves, let alone the broader organisation. The Amazon *two pizza rule*, where project teams should be small enough to be fed by two pizzas, is now famous. There obviously comes a point when projects become established and have grown to the point where more formal infrastructure and resource are required, but that is once projects have achieved market traction. Prior to that, innovation requires speed and so the smaller the team the better – small teams drive breadth of expertise as well as broad stakeholder buy-in.

Case example: Small team moving fast at Sky News

I was working at Sky News and we wanted to mark the anniversary of British service men and women in Afghanistan, as 200 people had died. So the Head of News got some of the key people in a room and in 15 minutes we brainstormed options and formed a plan. The idea was a digital cenotaph with the faces of all the fallen streaming up it. It went across all platforms and you could click on each picture and not just get the profile of the person but also the tributes from their parents and children and spouses. It was really moving. There were just five of us in a room and we built it in just three days off the back of a spreadsheet but it worked brilliantly and really captured the moment. We won an innovation award for it too.

Julian March, Former Head of Digital, Sky News

At the same time, the team needs to contain the necessary skills, knowledge and expertise to create a robust proposition. Depending on the organisational structure, this often means including representatives from technical, operational and finance functions, as well as the normal product or marketing people. In addition to ensuring the concept is robust from a functional standpoint, this also helps with engaging the core business. For example, if one of the finance team is creating the business case then the finance director will be kept abreast of developments by a trusted lieutenant, and be able to feed back through an informal trusted route rather than just discussing in more formal meetings with the project leader, who may tend to speak in more marketing or technical language, which could create friction.

Whilst small cross-functional teams are normally adept at moving quickly, this is only true if they are given the mandate to make their own decisions and act upon them. The reason they can move quickly is that they are not caught up in building consensus, then gaining approval from bureaucratic processes, and finally trying to engage other parts of the organisation to implement the decisions. They can just get on with it.

Case example: Small cross-functional teams delivering the Kindle at Amazon

The smartest thing I've seen done was the 1st generation Kindle project. It was a specific project that went very well because an effective multi-disciplinary team was established and you can't be led by a single function. It doesn't matter whether it's led by design, engineering or business – none of them work. It needs to be small, tight teams with key experts from each domain working together. There is always tension between the different functions and in this way it can be managed effectively upfront. Otherwise you just get pulled in one direction. The best companies recognise this and set up the right team right from the get-go.

At the early stage you need a balance between the doers and the strategy planners – but these guys need to know what it means to get things done. They need experience. This is where Amazon did so well around the Kindle. They got the right people together from the start and gave them the opportunity to go and do it.

Tom Hobbs, Former Creative Director, Teague

Case example: Small cross-functional team delivering exceptional results at Procter & Gamble

I joined a new team focusing on new brand development at P&G. We each got allocated three technologies as a team that we had to commercialise. It was a global function but a tiny team. One of my technologies was for getting rid of odours in Fabric Care. Our clever R&D teams managed to suspend it in a solution to help us address the consumer unmet need for cleaning difficult to wash fabrics. It became Febreze. The three test markets went well so, with competitive pressure, we decided to roll it out quickly and it went to 11 countries in 12 months, driving best practice rollout at pace and with efficiency.

We had absolute clarity on what we could and couldn't change. The rules of engagement were clear. So we didn't waste time fighting things you couldn't change, we just focused on things you could and that was very empowering. We did lots of consumer research and user acceptance so we knew there was a strong need and an excellent product. Behaviour change with consumers is really hard and we managed to focus on all those silly workarounds that people do and that actually our product was a far better answer. Consumers got that and it took off.

At that time, it was the fastest brand ever in P&G to reach the $1 billion turnover threshold. The reason it was successful was that we had a very tight small multidisciplinary team, consisting of R&D, Product Supply, Finance and Marketing. It meant doing lots of work outside our normal functions, being agile and focused, all joined up behind one vision with very quick decision-making and it was great fun. Being small, focused and multidisciplinary made it much easier.

Dean Keeling, Former Marketing Director, Shopper Marketing, Procter & Gamble

---

Team diversity is important

A cross-functional team is important, but just ticking a box that the team has representatives from the key departments is not enough. For real creativity and to avoid having a very skewed impression of the world, diversity within the team is needed too. This means having women as well as men, old as well as young, people from a range of economic and social backgrounds, staff who have worked their way up as well as new graduates, and so on. It is very common for a team to come up with propositions and features that reflect their own perspectives, and so many propositions are often targeted at affluent, middle class, middle aged men – because that's what the majority of people in the majority of head offices are. Or they are too forward thinking, because the innovation team is formed of innovators whose mindset doesn't match that of the mass market. And when they do work on projects targeting other segments, they are rarely as well thought through because the understanding of the customers and the market just isn't there. Therefore, the broader the range of backgrounds on the team the better.

❝ Commonly, you get too many early adopters **in an innovation team –** they jump on trends too early and the idea fails. **Not just that, it makes the idea taboo** so then they miss it when it actually happens. **❞**

**Tim Thorne, Chief Innovation &
Disruption Officer, TAL**

Diversity does not just apply to backgrounds, but also to personality traits. A number of studies into personality types for creativity and innovation have revealed some interesting patterns. Some of the most famous innovators – such as Bill Gates, Steve Jobs and Warren Buffett – all show a similar personality type, which is ENTJ on the Myers-Briggs Type Indicator (MBTI). Further research (Stevens and Burley, 1993) has claimed that the NT indicators from the MBTI test are key attributes of successful innovators. Indeed, the research showed a significant performance difference for these types that led to a far more effective and efficient team where NTs are deployed. A number of studies (Bouchard 1990 and 1993, Rosen 1987, Stassen 1992 and 1994, and Wolfe 1996) have also shown that these personality types are effectively genetic, implying that innovation and creativity cannot be taught effectively to those who do not possess the right attributes.

Whilst this points to some important criteria, it must not be forgotten that different skill sets suit different stages of the innovation life-cycle. It is common to think of innovation departments as being full of the wacky guys who come up with fantastic new ideas. Yes, you need some of those types, but innovation is far more about developing an idea than having the idea in the first place, and so different skill sets come into play as ventures develop. Whilst it would be great to have a Steve Jobs in the team, it is unlikely you would want a whole team of them.

Case example: Diverse perspectives enabling new category creation at Philips

There was an insight that in Northern Europe it's hard for people to wake up in winter. The reality is that when the sun rises, it sets off a chemical reaction in the brain to wake up. So in the winter when it's dark and the alarm clock goes off, people are not physically prepared to wake up. So we created a wake up light which had a bulb that comes on faintly 30 minutes before the alarm and gets stronger. This created a new category around a very strong performing consumer insight.

The technology existed in the organisation for some time in the Research and Development team, and it took off once the marketers played with it. Sometimes R&D teams think an idea is too technical or complex but when they start to work closely with marketers and other teams to build something, it takes a different perspective or way of looking at an insight to actually spot the opportunity.

Georgina Schiffers, Former General Manager, Active Play, Philips

Teams benefit from working together in the same practical space

A common debate when establishing a new innovation programme is the location and space that the team will work in. Companies often like to back up the idea of being creative and thinking differently to the normal business by investing in a more creative workspace, often with brightly covered offices, beanbags and table football. Whilst the intention behind this is sound, the reality of the solution is short-sighted. The purpose of a different space is exactly that, to be different. Creating a funky space for a team is different, but only for a short period and then it too becomes the norm for that team and the issue of over-familiarity arises again.

Far more beneficial is for the team to frequently visit new spaces. The important thing is to be away from the desk, the laptop, the mobile, and seeing new things that might spark new ideas, be it in customers' homes, the customer service centre, the park, or a shopping mall.

"Space – utter waste of money. Yes, grey walls don't necessarily contribute but how does that turn into wacky offices. I saw at a blue-chip company an innovation room with astroturf floors, crazy decor and an expensive full size photo on the walls that they changed every quarter. The reality is that these rooms are rarely used and in fact I see it as a clear indicator that a company doesn't know about commercial innovation. Communication is very important and that's why space like a central communal kitchen is so important."

Meldrum Duncan, Co-Founder, Curious Industry

Furthermore, investment in different spaces that on the one hand may be seen as cool and creative can backfire if employees in the core organisation see it as unfair and wasted money. This can obviously be one of the factors in undermining relations between the innovation team and the core. What can be helpful is a space that raises awareness of what the team are working on and striving for. This may be a permanent space if at a central site or potentially established as a roadshow if a number of locations are involved. Helping staff in the core division understand the technologies that are being worked on, the trends driving market changes and the vision can be far more useful in securing support from the core organisation than a funky armchair.

❝Projects rely on communication. There is a half-life of communication of about 50 feet, so people need to be pushed together. You can't innovate over email. ❞

Dave Wardle, Former Global Technology Manager, BOC

It is important that the team is located together, though whether that is onsite with the rest of the core staff or at a separate location may need to be decided by the overall purpose of the programme and its level of focus on the core business. Staff in innovation teams need to work alongside each other to speed up knowledge sharing and decision-making. Whether at a separate location or not, investment is better spent on normal office space and getting the team out of the building regularly than on a 'creative' space that will soon grow tired.

Summary

〜〜〜> **Successful innovation requires a dedicated and specialist team operating in the right culture** – The team must be experienced and possess the right skills and attitudes. Also, they need to be totally focused on the programme and given the right cultural environment for success.

〜〜〜> **Small cross-functional teams drive breadth of expertise as well as broad stakeholder buy-in** – Teams need to be small and selected from the right functions to enable successful delivery.

〜〜〜> **Team diversity is important** – A mix of different backgrounds and personality traits drives broader perspectives and skill sets on to the development and evolution of new ideas.

〜〜〜> **These teams benefit from working together in the same practical space** – Innovation teams need the right space, but that is not comfortable sofas and table football. It is a space where the team are all together to enable focus, and if looking for ideas then it's a space that encourages interaction with other employees, stakeholders and customers.

Delivering Innovation Projects

Section B

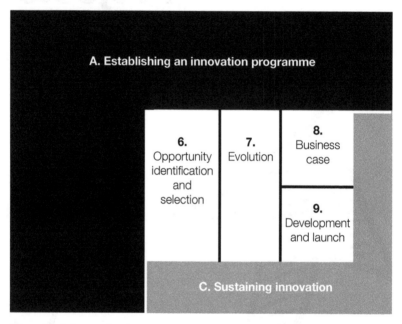

Figure B.1: Innovation framework

Section A focused on establishing an overall programme of innovation in the right way and creating the environment for success. However, even if this has been done in the best possible way, there are still many obstacles for individual projects to overcome and sadly many companies focus on the wrong things when delivering individual innovation projects.

Once an idea has been chosen for development, the real hard work begins. A large amount of work is required to define the proposition in detail, research with customers, define the pricing, design the product or service, understand the operational delivery and supply chain, work out the sales and service approach, build the required IT changes and prototypes, create a marketing plan, develop the business case and trial or pilot the idea, and all of the above will need a number of iterations.

Much of the above is just hard work, attention to detail and an ability to retain focus on delivering the MVP. However, in the corporate environment, delivering innovation also means understanding the implications of the vision, what it is trying to achieve and the implications on the core business. If all of this is not recognised early on, it can create far greater obstacles.

Figure B.1 shows a modified version of the innovation framework diagram, with section B on delivering innovation projects broken down into its principal constituent areas.

The chapters of Part B discuss these sub-sections within delivering innovation.

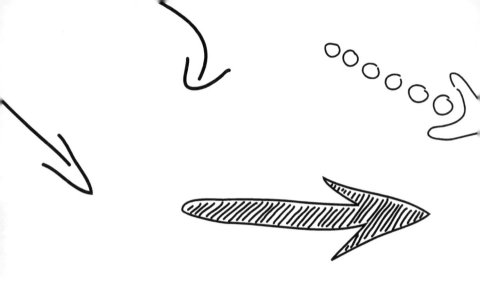

" Most corporate innovation doesn't fall over **because of a lack of passion,** or vision, or quality people, but because **they misinterpret what needs to be true** to deliver it. **"**

**Dean Keeling, MD UK,
Domestic & General**

6. Opportunity Identification and Selection

Focus on the customer problem, not the idea or the technology, to identify opportunities.

Understand the customer's problem

Some companies have an idea and want to get it in front of customers quickly, but they do this before they have even talked to customers about the problem.

Rather than being randomly generated from a top-down strategy process or from blue sky brainstorming techniques, compelling ideas address a specific problem experienced by customers. This means that successful idea generation starts with deep insight into the customer segment, their behaviours and attitudes, and the exact nature of the problem and its context.

It sounds obvious that only when the problem is viewed with real clarity can the solution be delivered, and yet it is common to see corporate teams struggling to pin down the core of a proposition, simply because the problem they are trying to solve is not fully understood.

It is far easier to come up with ideas against a specific question than it is to generate ideas for a totally blank canvas. A clear problem statement is a great start point for generating ideas, but more importantly, those ideas will be resolving an important issue by definition, and hence are likely to be far more robust than blue sky thinking.

It is also important to make sure that the problem being focused on is worth solving for customers. A lot of issues may exist, but there are only a few that a customer is actually going to pay extra for, or switch suppliers to resolve.

Case example: Identifying the real problem – the brief

I was working on a soup project in the Netherlands, where they drink the stuff like we drink coffee. The project was looking at NPD on new varieties. We'd tried sweeter, stronger, thicker, more-exotic, less-exotic and fusion but none of it grabbed the attention of consumers plus we had some fears about cannibalisation. So we stopped the project.

We stepped back and found that actually the challenge was making sure that consumers had ready access to soup, so it suddenly became a channel project. We came up with a water boiler and proposition that turned every newsagent in the land into a vendor. It was wildly successful and opened around 3000 new outlets for the brand. People think of innovation as NPD, when in fact it's about problem solving.

Meldrum Duncan, Co-Founder, Curious Industry

Case example: Clarifying the customer and commercial problem to innovate at BT

How do you grow the market in mature consumer telephony?

BT Answer 1571 was a spectacularly successful project but was still really hard to get over the line when it launched. Essentially, 40% of all call attempts ended in either no reply or the busy tone, which meant we were missing out on a lot of revenue and the customers were missing out on a lot of conversations.

So we came up with the idea of the 1571 service as a way of addressing it. The product line approached our technology supplier, who had actually already launched a similar product for Telefonica in Spain and they were able to give us lots of advice about the way to do it. The issue was around the commercials and the fear of cannibalization – the model was to offer it free and then charge the caller a minimum of 5p for the answering service. The finance community were worried that our 1.5 million paying voicemail customers would stop paying and just use this service and that we wouldn't get to the 4 or 5 million customers that we need to make the business case stack up. I had to fight tooth and nail to get it launched, but eventually the Retail CEO got behind the idea and then it moved quickly. Once launched it blew our expectations and hit over 7m users and drove lots of revenue that wouldn't have been there – effectively opening up that 40% of the market that wasn't previously available and growing the market by turning non-calls into calls. It all happened because we dug into the problem and understood how we could solve it.

Ian Price, Former General Manager, Core Business, BT

Observe the real world first-hand to understand attitudes, behaviours and needs

One of the main factors that determines whether customer research is insightful is the extent to which it is combined with real-life observation. Getting a written response to a survey is obviously worse than speaking to a customer on the phone, which in itself is less informative than speaking with them face to face, when the researcher can get a much better sense of the answer as visual cues come into play. However, all of these pale in comparison to truly observing a customer's practical behaviour.

Sometimes for an innovation to be successful it will require customers to change their normal behaviour, which can be immensely challenging. You may have the best product in the world but if it needs the customer to do something different to their normal routine – whether in buying or using it – it can be far harder to achieve success. This reality makes customer observation even more important, as it's far easier to build a proposition that accounts for consumer behaviours if you fully understand them in the first place, as shown in the Procter & Gamble example on page 80.

So, the only way to achieve a real understanding of the problem is to get out of the building. Go and talk to customers, work with staff on the frontline, listen in on customer service calls, and spend time doing it to understand the context, the behaviours, the expectations, the attitudes and prejudices as well as just the stated needs. This does not mean asking a research agency to go and do it for you before handing you a report or video. It means you.

Some of us are more comfortable and interested than others in this, but the level of empathy and understanding that results is critical. Equally, it pays to think about how to involve key stakeholders and decision makers in this insight work too. If they understand the problem, then they are equally going to understand the answer. Ideally, that means involving them in the hands-on insight work as well, but if this isn't possible then vox-pops, film recreations and even bringing customers in and putting them in front of senior executives can bring it to life instead.

Case example: Really understanding the problem for a consumer goods innovation

In one piece of research on floor cleaning, I was interviewing a woman in her home but was struggling to get to the heart of the matter. So I offered to wash her floor while she watched. She was horrified that I did it wrong and we then had a really insightful conversation about what was important in floor cleaning. Any idea generation process can work, if you have the right person. It's not about validation but about getting to the bottom of the problem and hence the solution. Very rarely does an idea come from a brainstorm. It needs to be based on real-world experience.

Meldrum Duncan, Co-Founder, Curious Industry

One of my own favourite examples was working at British Gas looking at people's understanding of their energy bills as we examined how to roll out smart meters. As part of this project, we decided to go and visit some customers in their homes and interview them to get a real feel for how the household worked. We went to one flat, and were invited in for a coffee. The man considered himself fairly savvy and had found the cheapest energy supplier on one of the comparison sites. However, he still thought his energy bill was expensive, feeling that all of the Big 6 energy companies in the UK were the same and were profiteering. We sat with him for an hour going through this relatively standard response – if this had been on the phone then we would have learned very little.

However, for the whole hour that we were in his kitchen the heating was on, as it was winter, and the patio door was open. I was literally watching him complain about the cost of his bill and blaming it on the energy companies as he was unknowingly paying to heat the south London atmosphere. The customer problem in this instance was one of understanding; he wanted to reduce and manage his bill, but thought that he just needed the cheapest supplier.

There is another important benefit to embedding the gathering of customer insight into your own team rather than outsourcing to a traditional research agency. Traditionally, you would brief an agency on the questions that need answering and they would come back a few weeks later with a report on the answers. The issue is that the questions tend to change significantly during those few weeks as the hypotheses evolve and suddenly the market research is no longer relevant. However, by embedding the insight function and using rapid response tools that can provide customer insight in hours rather than weeks, the questions can evolve in tandem with the project thinking and provide far more meaningful results. There is also the benefit of gaining a far deeper customer understanding through being in the room rather than reading a PowerPoint report.

It can be hard in these first customer interviews to spot the common customer problems, not because there are not common problems, but because it is rare at this stage to have a tight enough definition of which customers are the focus. Entering these interviews with clear hypotheses, about the segments and their attitudes and needs, helps focus the lessons and clarify the results. It may therefore require two or three rounds of interviews, each more focused on a specific segment than the last, in order to get a proper understanding of the target segment and the customer problem.

Case example: Learning from frontline staff at Heathrow Airport

For us, walking not just in the customers' shoes but also those of our staff is fundamental. Not only does it really help their engagement and improve our understanding of the issues, but sometimes it can have real direct benefits too. Here at the airport, it's all about getting people through the various security checks as quickly as possible. One of the things we have to do is take a photo of passengers at the first checkpoint, which is done for families and passengers with reduced mobility by pointing a simple webcam. This is fine for adults, but children always shy away and it takes time to get them to look into the camera. That costs 20-30 seconds every time a child comes through. One of the security officers had the idea to use the picture of the cartoon plane that was on some of our marketing materials and stick it on top of the camera, he just said look at the plane – kids step closer to get a look at it and he got a great picture every time with no delay. So now, all of our family lanes have a little plane on top of the camera. For the cost of the picture of a plane, we are saving lots of time and money. God knows what would have happened if we'd created a project team to solve that problem, I am sure they would never have come up with that.

Richard Harding, Interim Head of IT Strategy & Innovation, Heathrow

Case example: Observing the problem at
Baxter Renal

We were working on an observation project in dialysis clinics for this manufacturer of therapeutic equipment. One thing we observed was that nurses always carried a chart and a pen to make notes when they checked the machines. The thing was they used the wall or the bed to write on. So our client added a writing shelf on to the machine which was cheap to manufacture, but it added massive value, so the client was able to charge a few hundred dollars for it. This turned out to be the most popular accessory for the machine and it saved time and reduced mis-recordings of data and delivered significant revenue upside.

John Mitchell, Principal, Applied Marketing Science

Case example: Getting real world exposure at
major CPG multinational

They took 12 of us out of the business for six weeks. The first two weeks was pure immersion. We met customers, retailers, professors – lots of people giving us great understanding. That plus just having the time to discuss it meant we got not just a lot of ideas (1500) but also some great ones too – when we prioritized down to the top 15 and took a snapshot of them they scored unbelievably well against our normal criteria. For example, we'd been chatting with a pregnant woman and it just happened that I commented about how my gums had bled when I'd been pregnant. One of our technical experts was with us and it turns out that's really common and a natural condition, and from that we had an idea around doing a pregnancy test. That's now been launched, but we'd never have thought of that if we hadn't had this immersion with the time to develop our thinking and the right skills in the room like technical and marketing and legal to understand it. It's all about immersing a cross-functional team and giving the space and focus to just work it.

Jaime Kalfus, Former Global Strategy Director, Red Fuse Communications

Be naïve

Curiosity is often referenced as one of the key attributes for successful innovators. The desire to really understand how things work and how they could be better is a great mindset to have. Over time curiosity can be dulled, particularly if somebody has stayed in the same role and organisation for a long period and so, along with a natural curiosity, there is a need for an element of naivety. Sometimes people don't ask questions about why things are the way they are because some aspects are so ingrained in the culture, they've always been done that way. It takes somebody with a naïve curiosity to ask apparently stupid questions, only to find that nobody knows the answer and there is a great opportunity to improve something.

Case example: Naïve curiosity creating new opportunities at British Airways

I worked on the first flat bed in business class for British Airways Club World. As a naïve 31-year-old design executive, I can remember just saying to the brand manager, 'We need to sort Club World! – what if we offered the first flat bed in business class?' It was a child-like naïve question. I'm sure lots of smart people had had the idea before, but nobody perhaps had the courage to ask the question. Normally hierarchy and fear of failure stops questions being asked. It was that corridor conversation not a formal meeting that ignited the energy for the programme. I asked because I cared. Virgin Atlantic already had a slanting bed design and we needed to respond and surpass. The brand manager responded positively, so too his team, and it just snowballed from there. In the early stages of the programme, senior management were catching up with us as we just got on and did it. People came on board. It was a genuine, meaningful innovation that drove competitive advantage on BA's crucial north Atlantic routes, which was the core of the business at the time.

Paul Wylde, Founder & Creative Director, PaulWylde

Naivety is not just about asking silly questions. My four-year-old does that. But what my four-year-old also does, is go and try things that he doesn't understand or realise what the consequences might be. Likewise, sometimes we would never launch a new venture if we realised how hard it was going to be or some of the implications of it. Yet, once it is done and you have resolved those unforeseen issues, great things can come from it.

b

Case example: Being naïve enough to launch at BOC

I was in the US between '96 and 2000, and we started a data business purely driven through innovation process. We extracted data from customers' manufacturing lines and analysed and then sold the data and insights back to them. We developed the vision, got buy-in and got great response. We were naïve doing it and didn't realise how hard it was. We would never have done it if we'd known how hard it would be. The ridiculous thing was that the core business wanted to give it away for free in order to keep the commodity business going. They were trying to save a dying and barely profitable business by giving away this great revenue opportunity. But the core always has a strong voice and it was a tough negotiation and a good reason to set up skunk works with a firewall between the core business and the innovation.

Dave Wardle, Former Global Technology Manager, BOC

Don't start with the technology or capability

Big businesses are full of ideas, but not all of them are equal. Some have come about because they fit a particular strategy or are based on a capability or technology that the company has access to. These ideas are effectively a solution looking for a problem and can only really work if a genuine customer need can be identified that they address. This is dangerous, as there is too often a desire to twist the evidence or insight from customers to fit the solution. It is only natural to have bias towards the shiny new idea. Worse still, this bias means that there may well be a strong customer problem or opportunity that should be addressed which is then ignored as the project is focused on finding a home for its pre-conceived idea. So whilst these technologies and capabilities can be great assets and differentiators when launching new products and services, they should not be the starting point.

Case example: Innovating from a customer rather than technology perspective with global make-up brand

We were talking with people in the make-up industry, and they were telling us that there is a certain age group that just go out with their make-up compact. So we looked at how we could include payment, and figured out we could embed a chip. That is a new form factor and experience. You're not building from scratch but it is a new use case appealing to a different segment. These sorts of opportunities can often get overlooked, because teams just get more excited about new technology rather than solving for the customer needs.

Ruth Whitten, VP International Markets, MasterCard

Do not over-invest in idea generation

Idea generation is easy and too much time and focus is often given to the idea generation phase of a project. Typically, a standard innovation programme will come up with far more ideas than the organisation can possibly deliver. Some will be incremental ideas, some disruptive, some wacky, and some old ideas that have been heard before (although this does not necessarily mean that they are no good). Whilst easy, there are still ways of optimising the process to match the programme's objectives, and some pitfalls to avoid.

There are countless ways of generating ideas from co-creation, to hackathons, to idea submission schemes, to classic brainstorms (or silent brainstorms for the introverts amongst us), or even just a look through a list of customer complaints. Many of these are based around a few core approaches, but different idea generation techniques will tend to lead to certain types of idea. For example, reviewing a competitor's product to try and better it will tend to focus on a new set of product features, whereas a hackathon will tend to result in a new app. With this in mind it is important to select the right type of idea generation techniques that will come up with ideas that meet the programme objectives.

b

Whilst ideas may come from a wide range of places, the most important element in the potential success of the idea is understanding the customers and their behaviours, needs and frustrations. If the idea can clearly address an important need or frustration for a specific customer group then it typically merits further investigation.

There are a few basic factors beyond using the right idea generation technique that will enhance your chances of success:

➤ **Involve the right people in the process** – It doesn't matter whether it's top executives or frontline staff, co-creation with customers or staff from back-office support functions, there are a few key attributes that make some people better suited than others, typically those with natural optimism, who can see the big picture. It may be useful to include a subject-matter expert, but putting a whole group of them together is rarely successful.

➤ **Get help** – Get professional external facilitators. It's worth it and allows the innovation team to focus on innovation rather than facilitation.

➤ **Go beyond the usual** – Every organisation has a handful of ideas that have been hanging around at the watercooler for ages. Get these out on the table before entering into serious idea generation. That way, staff know that they have been heard and are challenged to move on. Likewise, find ways of pushing the ideas outside of the normal comfort zone: use scenarios, extreme situations, competitive war games, role plays, and agitators – whatever it takes. That liberates people to think beyond the norm and stretch ideas as far as they will go.

➤ **Engage senior stakeholders early** – Involve all relevant people in the process, even if they do not meet the desired attributes above or are naysayers. Their contribution can still be valuable and this prevents them from later claiming that they were not consulted. Quite the opposite – this can be the first step in getting them on-board with the programme. This does not necessarily mean involving them in the idea generation process, but rather involve them in a review process before much development is done. This can flush out any pet ideas they may have and also highlight any problem areas early on. Maintaining this involvement throughout the development process is fundamental to success.

The one most common and most serious pitfall in idea generation is failing to clarify what the concept really is. Short templates are often completed in fairly haphazard fashion as it's not the most fun part of idea generation and so the core idea within the concept is often not fully understood and rarely is there a shared understanding of it across the team. This can lead to very different views of whether a concept is good or not, and great concepts can be lost through a lack of clarity. Therefore, it is worth taking the time to challenge each idea and get to the heart of it as a team before casting judgement. This is particularly true where the problem that you're trying to solve isn't understood with sufficient clarity, as discussed earlier in this chapter.

Case example: Pushing the envelope at
JetBlue

First you have to create the conditions for success.

Then you need the methods and system for creativity – permission to ask silly questions. You always have to throw the ball way out, reach for the clouds to take a step forwards. For example, when we came up with the Gourmet Galley for JetBlue, we started out thinking about giving the area to one of the big food companies like Whole Foods, but that was too much, so then it came out to being radical ourselves with fridges and microwaves and so on and that was still too much so we came down to a destination snack bar. What BMW call, most advanced yet acceptable (MAYA). This liberates creativity and curiosity and allows you to ask questions in a safe environment.

Paul Wlyde, Founder & Creative Director, PaulWylde

Idea co-creation

Sometimes customers can have a role in helping create the idea itself. Co-creation is becoming an increasingly popular tool, and can be effective in certain situations if used in the right way. Normally if you ask a customer for ideas, they will tend to base their thinking on their existing knowledge of your product and so you get customer experience and product improvements, or things which they have seen competitors do. That is to say, they are great for incremental ideas.

To go beyond this, customers tend to benefit from stimuli that will stretch their thinking beyond that context, but as the stimuli are often already subjective based on whoever has produced them, it can be a frustrating and misleading exercise. That said, there is a great example below from Henkel, where the company already had an interesting idea, but couldn't get a good positioning with customers, a problem that the customer themselves soon solved.

> ## Case example: Co-creation for successful automatic dishwasher detergent in Henkel Germany
>
> There was intrinsic growth in the market as dishwashing machines were increasing in penetration so there was 10% organic market growth. Henkel was the leader with 50% market share, then Benckiser with 30% and Unilever's Sun has around 10%. The market was mainly in powders at this stage though Henkel had a tablet. Then P&G decided to enter by bringing Fairy into the machine market. This was a massive threat to the incumbents.
>
> At Benckiser, we had an idea for a 2 layer tablet, which came from another category. There was actually only one technical benefit from the 2 layers, which was that it extended the shelf-life of the cleaning performance as it separated the enzymes and the cleaning agent which otherwise would erode each other. The division CEO really believed in the idea and signed off the ideas very early on, and then told marketing to go and sell it.
>
> We tested the concept and it bombed and researched worse than our existing product. Consumers just weren't interested in the messages that it still cleaned brilliantly after 5 weeks. So we chose a bottom-up approach to developing the concept, which meant giving the tablet to a series of focus groups and seeing what they made of it. We let them define it and how to sell it and then we took their ideas into the next focus group. We iterated this process 4 times to get 3 or 4 concepts that went to quantitative research. It turned out, that they wanted to know which part of the tablet did what, so the white bit does the cleaning and blue layer gave the superior shine for which our brand was famous. Suddenly, customers loved it and we achieved market leadership over both Henkel and P&G's Fairy.
>
> At the end of the day, the product wasn't that different but the different look gave customers a way of understanding the different functions and we communicated in consumer language rather than the technical benefits.
>
> **Andreas Welsch, Former Marketing Director, Benckiser**

Leveraging trend analysis

Within the opportunity identification and selection phase, it can sometimes be helpful to identify the trends and hotspots where change is occurring more quickly. Some companies establish teams to scan market trends by investigating new technologies or examining the investment trends in venture capital, whilst others will carry out foresight projects to try to understand broader trends in society and their potential impacts. All of these approaches have their place and can bring insight, inspiration and confidence, but they need to be applied within the context of the overall purpose.

These trends can help identify themes and areas of opportunity to focus on for idea generation and create a strong context for the ideas that begin to emerge from the programme. Most importantly, and as demonstrated by the Alfa example below, looking at trends and precedents from around the world in this way gives teams not just the insight and the inspiration, but also the confidence to go ahead.

b

Delivering Innovation Projects

Case example: Using consumer trends and innovation examples to drive innovation at Alfa Bank

Trends are a great source of inspiration. When we look for trends we look at signals – things that have unlocked or newly serviced an existing consumer need or desire.

By applying consumer trends to your business to turn opportunities into innovation, you make sure you don't create for the sake of creation but ground your new products and services into what your customers really need – innovating in a meaningful way.

For example, 42 Agency, a Moscow-based advertising agency, came up with a new product for Alfa Bank which is the largest private commercial bank in Russia. In a workshop session, they applied one of our trends – 'Currencies of Change': brands that incentivized improving behaviours with rewards and benefits* – and created 'Activity' – an app that uses fitness trackers like Fitbit, Jawbone UP or RunKeeper to transfer small amounts of money to customers' savings accounts based on how much they exercise. The fitness trackers move savings into an account that has a 6% interest rate – the only way they can access that high rate. It was really only by looking at trends and precedents this way, that they had both the inspiration and the confidence to go ahead.

*For example, AirBaltic linked the miles flown by travellers to a target for burning calories, with an airmiles reward for passengers achieving their target and Nike's #makeitcount campaign lets FuelBand owners purchase products with earned Fuel points.

Delia Dumitrescu, Lead Innovation Architect, trendwatching.com

---

Kill bad ideas quickly

Once a large number of ideas have been generated – which might be anything from 20 to hundreds, depending on the scale of the programme – selection and prioritisation will be required to determine which ones will be worked on. This is a surprisingly easy task. Once lined up against the broad purpose of the innovation programme, many ideas can be eliminated due to their potential scale or focus, and whilst many processes still try to use some simple criteria at this stage, gut-feel of experienced intrapreneurs can be very effective at selecting the best ideas.

There are really two main lenses through which to consider idea prioritisation:

1. Does the idea have good potential as an idea? For this, I often consider the four elements of the *decision diamond*:

➤ *Customer resolution* – Is there a clear and strong customer problem that this idea resolves better than alternatives?

➤ *Viability* – Does the likely business model and cost-benefit equation make commercial sense?

➤ *Do-ability* – Is it technically and operationally possible?

➤ *Scalability* – Does it have potential to scale successfully from market size, viability and feasibility perspectives?

2. **Is the idea appropriate for the current context?** The answer to the above questions may be positive, but it still may not be appropriate to progress the opportunity for a range of reasons, such as strategy and brand.

Figure 6.1 illustrates the first of these points – the area where desirability, viability, feasibility and scalability meet.

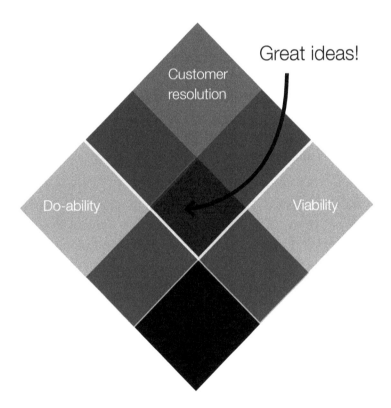

Figure 6.1. Idea selection – the decision diamond

Whatever approach is used, there is no need to overcomplicate it or divert too much time and effort to it, as long as the stakeholders are engaged and aligned.

"The best projects are those that are small enough that it doesn't matter if they fail, but can grow into something meaningful if they work."

Andrew Harris, Director of Deposits, Barclays

Some companies will fret over ignoring a potentially great idea. The truth is that it just doesn't matter. The key to this process is enabling the business to focus in on a few ideas that it has the capacity to handle and deliver. The objective of the prioritisation is therefore simply to identify the best few ideas to take forward. Other ideas are not necessarily lost, they will just have to wait their turn. As stated above, identifying ideas is easy, and there is no need to get hung up on a single one. This process of natural selection is important in weeding out bad ideas, pet projects and helping the team focus in on the few best ones.

Sometimes, bad ideas still get through and it is important to kill bad ideas quickly without wasting lots of time and resource on making them work. This can be difficult, particularly if a stakeholder backs the project and it's in danger of becoming a pet project.

In identifying the best ideas, it's also important to make sure that they will not fall foul of easy challenges. Many *new* ideas have been thought of before, often within the same organisation, and there is almost always somebody who will explain that "We've tried that before and it didn't work...". Not checking this early on can risk either a good idea getting shut down for the wrong reasons or, equally poor, repeating the same mistakes that have been made before.

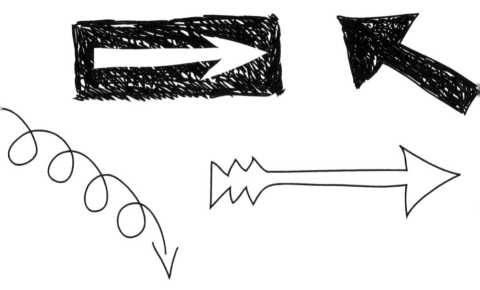

❝ It goes wrong when there is a really bad idea **that nobody is prepared to tell the CEO** is crap. There's an idea that was never any **good but somebody wants to do it and** so everybody just does their bit without *any real effort and it comes out half-baked.* **❞**

Michael Johnson, Former MD
New Ventures, Which?

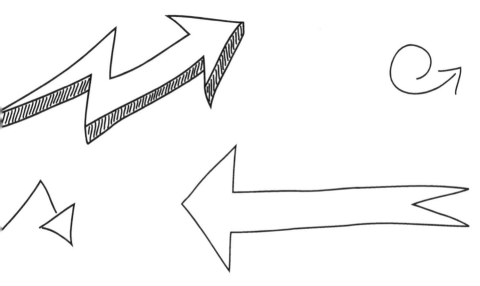

Create a reason to believe

Companies will identify hundreds if not thousands of opportunities and many of these will have sound reasons for pursuing them, but equally it can be very easy to say no to new ideas. Most organisations are set up for the default answer to change to be "no". Whether it is because the idea is too small or too risky, or too costly, or does not exactly match the strategic direction, or even just because it hasn't captured the imagination of the stakeholders, it can easily fail to get investment. Therefore, at the very outset of innovation projects, it is necessary to identify a reason for the stakeholders to believe in the project.

Case example: Gaining support for innovation at ICI

There are some key elements to actually delivering innovation. The ability to work well across boundaries is fundamental, and we got great results when we focused a diverse team on a single big challenge. Of course, it is important to iterate ideas rapidly to keep stretching them and finding where the bigger ideas lie. The worst thing though is launching by committee. Everybody chips away at things and you end up with a very average innovation. That's why a lot of innovation is about internal cut-through in the early stages. I was at a meeting where one of the brands wanted to get stakeholder attention for their idea. They created a mock-up of a trade journal announcing that the idea had just been launched as a new product by one of their major competitors. It made the conversation suddenly become serious and the project got approval quickly. You have to think about your stakeholders and be creative about getting their attention. Of course the flipside of this is that you can spend more time on materials for internal committees than on the innovation itself. You have to be creative and quick and use external help.

Mary Ward, Former Innovation Director, UK, ICI Paints

Tell a story that engages the right brain as well as the left

Often companies will be biased towards certain decision-making criteria, so for example some organisations will be very commercial, others strategic and others brand-led. Whilst this will influence the style of dialogue in deciding on projects, it is rare that all decision makers will be biased in the same way. For this reason, it's necessary to cover both the rational strategic and commercial reasons for going ahead with the project, as well as the more inspirational reasons that look to what the organisation, product or world could look like if given the green light. This will capture the imagination of stakeholders.

There are countless articles dedicated to the principles around storytelling and how to engage the heart and mind, thinking and feeling, from an audience, but there are some specifics to the situation of the corporate entrepreneur.

Given the variety of stakeholders, it may be necessary to tailor the story to different audiences. The finance director may need a story that leads with the numbers but still pulls at the emotions, whereas the marketing director may respond to a real customer example of how the idea might transform their experience. Feeding in real and current issues can ensure that the story resonates. Again, the story may lead with different issues subject to the audience.

As always, having a clear call to action is important, and it is easy to fall into the trap of selling the concept and for the request to be to go ahead with it. Far better is to position it in terms of the innovation process, and for the project to be taken to the next phase to be explored further. This means that a green light is just for the next stage of discovery or a test rather than a full launch. This gives confidence that the project is being properly managed, with a process in place to address issues and concerns, and with further opportunity to discuss it later.

b

Case example: Creating the emotional case for overseas expansion at Sainsbury's

I was looking at whether Sainsbury's should go abroad. Sainsbury's had very limited experience of international markets so this was a big deal and we took the entire board to China for a week. It was like due diligence on the country and we saw experts from real estate, advertising agencies, consumer insights, banks, logistics and the supply chain. We went through all the numbers and whilst this may have worked for the CFO and Operations Director, it didn't do it for the Marketing Director or CEO. But two moments changed this:

1. We went with the founder of a local supermarket chain for a tour round his supermarkets. This gave a real insight into the way things were done, and the CEO and sceptical others began to see how Sainsbury's would actually operate and work.

2. We got the equivalent of Jamie Oliver to talk about Chinese cooking, the four key ingredients and four key utensils that every home has. Again the board could suddenly see a purpose for Sainsbury's in this market – an ambition around healthy and tasty food – and what we'd need our experience to look like.

This was a hard sell, but seeing the vision for themselves, rather than just the numbers, made them buy in. So we got the green light for a team to go and look for acquisitions.

A major part of my work is involving senior leadership – they have to believe in it to do it. You need ambition or fear to drive it. Good ideas don't survive on their own merits. Whereas start-ups have the advantage here as they just need to get the buy-in of a handful of people and will just do it.

Jason Stanard, Former Head of Strategy, Sainsbury's

Tie the reason to believe back into the burning platform

Sometimes even having a strong reason to believe is not enough. Even if the project is viewed positively, there may be more urgent or important projects that need attention. Therefore, it will only be the point at which the project is tied back into the original burning platform that a sense of urgency to move forwards can be achieved.

Case example: Burning platform driving urgency at GSK

If necessity is the mother of invention, then competitive pressure can really create change and help decision-making in large companies. In 2011 we launched Sensodyne Repair and Protect, it went on to be one of the most successful product launches for GSK Consumer Healthcare in the past ten years. At the time, Sensodyne was the market leader but true market penetration was still relatively small. But with sensitive toothpastes sold at a decent price premium, it was attractive to everyone, including our competitors. We found a key insight that when people are in pain, a large group of them would prefer to get to the root cause and fix it, and were willing to pay more for this. So the concept of 'repairing and protecting' was born, to help fix rather than simply relieve pain. Coming from a credible trusted brand, people not only believed it would actually repair your teeth, but were also excited by the benefit. Landing this huge project had multiple financial, technical and decision-making challenges, all of which were sped up due to pressure coming from our key competitors. It's this competitive pressure that created a sense of urgency and momentum behind the product's launch, and ultimately its success.

Shafik Saba, Former Global Marketing Director, Sensodyne, GSK

Summary

➤➤ **Understand the customers' problem** – The best ideas address a clear and specific problem experienced by the customer.

➤➤ **Make sure YOU have first-hand, real-world insights** – Get out of the building and understand customer behaviour as well as their needs.

➤ **Be naïve** – Keep asking basic questions and trying new solutions.

➤ **Do not over-invest in idea generation** – A lot of ideas will come quickly, but make sure that you use the right techniques to maximise the chances of finding ideas that meet the programme objectives.

➤ **Idea co-creation has a role to play but use it in the right way** – Customers can help create new ideas, but use them for incremental enhancements.

➤ **Leveraging trend analysis can bring insight, inspiration and confidence to go ahead** – Trends, hotspots and precedents can fit within the strategy to provide insight into opportunities, inspiration for new ideas and confidence to proceed.

➤ **Kill bad ideas quickly** – Be ruthless and focus only on the best ideas.

➤ **Tell a story that engages the right brain as well as the left** – Get stakeholders engaged both emotionally and rationally.

➤ **Tie the reason to believe back into the burning platform** – Great ideas with good support can still be sidelined. Link them back to the burning platform to create a sense of urgency.

7. Evolution

Evolve concepts proactively rather than reactively.

"Whilst many companies have governance and process, they don't strategically manage them. Projects get in through the first stage-gate, and then only come out again if they fail. Projects should be constantly challenged, reviewed and readjusted. Otherwise, you may drift into an area and launch products that aren't ready or shouldn't be launched."

Dennis Nelson, Former R&D Director, Pfizer

Once idea generation is complete, there is still much development work to be done. Ideas normally change significantly as they develop and are often unrecognisable at the end of the process compared to the original idea. They may be combined with other ideas to make them bigger and better, and they will almost certainly have to adapt to a wealth of regulatory, technical, legal, operational and commercial challenges, leading to some fundamental changes to the original idea.

There are numerous examples of this: YouTube was originally a video dating site called Tune In Hook Up, whilst Groupon started out as a social media platform to bring people together to solve problems. Group buying only came about as an idea from people using the site. Meanwhile, Instagram began as a location checking and social diary application.

Rarely is an idea perfect from the start. It is not uncommon to have a great idea but be thinking about the wrong business model or customer group, as highlighted in the case example from clust. com below. Therefore, it is important to develop ideas and improve them as you and your team learn more about them.

Case example: Finding the right customer for Clust

A number of years ago in the dot.com era, I worked for a French company that was in group buying (a bit like today's Groupon). I was one of the first employees and I launched the retail brand in France. This was at the time of QXL and priceline and they were all based around dynamic pricing technology. Our mandate was international growth beyond France and we focused on the UK. But we found that another company (LetsBuyIt) was already doing that in UK. So we decided to step back and work out what we did well and how we could position ourselves. We realised we had logistics contracts, IT and buying teams – all the infrastructure you need which was just as useful in the B2B space as the B2C one. There was no significant competition in the B2B space so off we went. We added B2B sales and account management capabilities and worked with the likes of Virgin, Egg and the *Daily Telegraph* and this became a successful business. It was eventually sold to a French retailer.

Jason Stanard, Former UK MD, Clust

This development has to turn a simple idea, probably not much more than a couple of words on a Post-it note, into an attractive proposition that is easily conveyed to prospective customers – with a robust commercial model and clearly defined operating approach – and finally into a whole business that is ready to launch with all the support which that entails.

This involves the development of new processes, the writing of new code, the creation of new contracts, and recruitment of new people. The list goes on, and big business is typically not set up for this level of flexible building and testing at small-scale. The standard *change* processes which sit across the entire company will typically be slow, bureaucratic and unsympathetic towards these arduous but small-scale changes. Even in a lean methodology, there is a huge amount of work to be done.

Idea evolution should be proactive

Typically, good and bad ideas alike adapt to survive on their journey towards launch, whereas iteration should be about turning bad ideas into good ones and good ideas into great ones. Ideas will always need to evolve in the face of the various challenges that appear, whether they are technical, legal, operational, commercial or just customer feedback.

However, this evolution is normally on a crisis-driven basis: challenges arise so that the team then has to adapt the idea to resolve the problem. In this way, it is common for ideas to change significantly during their development from Post-it note to launched proposition, which is fine in itself, but often this evolution moves away from the original idea behind the concept, and unintentionally so.

Whilst these crisis-driven changes will always occur, a more proactive and less reactive system can be employed to keep the project aligned with its original purpose and drive improvements into the project as it progresses. There are a number of ways of doing this, but having regular proactive reviews of the proposition which seek to challenge its alignment to the customer needs and to the programme purpose are key. These reviews may include other stakeholders, teams, or even customers to challenge the project with a different perspective. Negative customer research feedback can be fully explored at these reviews as well as the usual operational and commercial challenges. In this way, iteration can

b

Delivering Innovation Projects

be delivered as a series of short-sprints that remain in the control of the innovation programme, rather than open-ended evolution in the face of the ad-hoc challenges that arise from outside the team.

This process of controlled iteration does not stop at launch, but should continue as real feedback comes from live customers, and management information is captured, in order to continue to learn lessons and improve the product in its early life.

Case example: Proactive iteration at Google

The best part of working on the web? We get do-overs. Lots of them. The first version of AdWords, released in 1999, wasn't very successful – almost no one clicked on the ads. Not many people remember that because we kept iterating and eventually reached the model we have today. And we're still improving it; every year we run tens of thousands of search and ads quality experiments, and over the past year we've launched over a dozen new formats. Some products we update every day.

Our iterative process often teaches us invaluable lessons. Watching users 'in the wild' as they use our products is the best way to find out what works, then we can act on that feedback. It's much better to learn these things early and be able to respond than to go too far down the wrong path.

Iterating has served us well. We weren't first to Search, but we were able to make progress in the market by working quickly, learning faster and taking our next steps based on data.

Susan Wojcicki, Google's Senior Vice President of Advertising, in 'The Eight Pillars of Innovation' (Google.com)

However, it should be noted that pivoting in a big business is potentially far harder than for start-ups. Stakeholders around the organisation will have bought into a particular vision and message about the proposition and their support can be undermined if the project is constantly shifting its focus and adjusting the proposition. For this reason, it is important to communicate the problem that is being addressed right from the start, as that will always be the anchor for the project, even if the proposition itself, the solution to the problem, evolves during the project.

b

Case example: Pivoting at E-Car Club

We've been more traditional in the research for E-Cars with focus groups and so on. Then three months post-launch we realized that lots of our assumptions were wrong and we had to pivot. In a corporate it's often hard to change direction quickly as you have already sold a message internally and it looks like you got it wrong. It takes a brave corporate investment committee to say 'just go and see what you can sell to the customer then work out the right business model from there'. Being material in a corporate means you have to define the (mythical) $1bn venture up front rather than constantly adapting in the face of reality; that makes it tough. That's far easier for us where we can focus on what's right for the customer rather than the right message to the investment committee.

Andrew Wordsworth, Executive Chairman, E-Car Club

Delivering Innovation Projects

Stay true to the proposition without compromise

One of the challenges that is particularly evident in the corporate environment is the tendency to water-down the original proposition idea as compromises are made along the way with various departments who are protecting their own turf. This can be anything from the finance team trying to improve the business case, or marketing trying to target other customers, or even just a senior stakeholder trying to blend in one of their own pet ideas or resolve one of their own issues.

Case example: Idea evolution for the wrong reasons at Henkel

The global instant adhesive market was a high margin market in decline in which Henkel was the market leader. Our divisional president believed in a new idea and set up the lines to deliver the product but the countries didn't believe in it and it was withdrawn after 15 months.

Typically, superglue comes in more quantity than is actually needed. Customers buy it, use it a couple of times and then it ends up drying out or being lost and getting thrown out. This idea was for a low-cost super glue for emerging markets where people couldn't afford such wastage. We found a smaller and cheaper way of packaging it so that it would become a 1-use product. This seemed a great idea but it evolved and got confused. Some countries started worrying about cannibalisation over the existing product and so they started manipulating the price to be higher, undermining the appeal. Then they started thinking about how to convince women to have an 'emergency glue' in their handbag, which is what the eventual marketing was based on.

By the end, none of the countries liked it, but the divisional president mandated it and pressured the countries into the launch. The value proposition had died as it moved from emerging markets to a convenience/ emergency just in case product. On paper it looked good, but not in reality and the CEO hadn't taken people with him. It also showed that you can't do everything centrally; you lose insight and HQ overestimate what consumers will want and exaggerate the problems they face. This lesson was further proven by the subsequent global brand relaunch that did get buy-in and was implemented by 50 countries in 12 months. This was successful and brought two years of over 10% sales and profit growth.

Andreas Welsch, Former SVP, Henkel

There is a constant pressure to compromise. If you're the operations manager you want a stable environment so that you can control it, yet everything an NPD or innovation team does is to create change and hassle. Innovation teams have got to stick to their principles rather than compromise. Often it is the finance department who want new propositions to be premium, or just to appeal to new customers rather than existing ones, which maximises the benefit by attracting new customers. The problem with doing this is that loyal customers are suffering and focus on the actual customer has been lost.

The constant nature of the pressure from all sides, often comprising suggestions for tweaks to the messaging or a new feature, or adding in another customer segment, brought against a simple idea that rarely has evidence or strong rationale to say no, means that the compromise can happen quickly and go relatively unnoticed until the project has launched.

It is all this compromise that means big businesses often launch new products that are either behind the market or simply underwhelming in their positioning.

b

Delivering Innovation Projects

ffInnovation teams have got to
stick to their principles
rather than compromise. **ЈЈ**

Case example: Proposition degeneration at Orange Australia

We were working on a great piece of technology and software that was built into the phone before the days of GPS that effectively turned your mobile phone into a local phone, so that when you were within 100 meters of your home, you could be charged at landline rates. I remember a senior director from the business arrived and said that his vision was for mobiles to take over home phones. He was really excited when we told him that we had the technology – which was a world first. Yet a year or so later as we came to launch, he along with the rest of the business were talking about it as a mobile phone proposition. Somehow it had gone through the business and turned into just another mobile phone tariff. The business owner needs to be left to get on with it. He's the passionate one on a mission to make it happen.

Michael Johnson, Former Marketing Director, Orange

Case example: Business case pressure impacting idea evolution at Ashland

It's very common at the early business case review stage to have the ideal product proposition. But as the final prototypes are developed you realize the costs are higher than the original business case assumptions. At this point you have a very critical decision to make – do you know if your customers are willing to pay more for this new product formula and benefit? We learned at Ashland Specialty Ingredients to have a check-in point with our strategic accounts in the prototype development phase so everyone involved understood the product costs and value proposition we were creating. It is more important to have those conversations with the customer at each stage of development than to realize too late in the process your costs are unacceptable and you cannot deliver the quality product the customer needs. An alternative is to develop the product at the lower cost range but then test this version and make sure it can deliver the same benefits as the original product promise.

Nancy Shea, VP, Global Innovation & Marketing, Ashland

Challenge all assumptions about the business

Most companies have their own way of doing things, based on a wide range of factors including their culture, processes, regulatory environment, traditions, people and management style. This way of doing things needs to be clearly understood by the corporate entrepreneur, not just to appreciate the context of the organisation and how to deliver projects within it, but also as an area of opportunity for new ideas and new processes that might enable successful innovation.

This way of doing things is a set of rules about what the organisation does and how it does it. The challenge is that some of these rules are real and there for good reason, but that is rarely the case for all of them and there are normally some unfounded assumptions which, if challenged, may unlock new opportunities. The trick is not just to understand which ones are real and which ones are not, but also to understand which ones might hold sufficient value to be worth challenging the established order over.

These assumptions can cover anything from what the company is all about, to who it serves and how it does it. We have seen British Telecom break the assumption that it was a telephony company and it is now completing a transformation into a media company. Whilst identifying assumptions to challenge can be a great source of ideas, it is also an important part of the delivery process, as illustrated in the Virgin Atlantic and ITV examples below.

b

Delivering Innovation Projects

Case example: Challenging assumptions at Virgin Atlantic

We were working on the business class seat that launched back in 2004. It was a revolution for us because it was the first time that business class had a seat and bed with two different surfaces. Previously we'd worried about how much pitch (room between the seats) we had rather than how many people you could fit into a cabin. We had always been constrained thinking about how to design a seat within a certain space and the passenger not moving, but on this project we managed to ask ourselves a bigger question. When we thought about the most efficient way for sleeping and sitting, we realized we'd have to go outside the conventional approach. Once we accepted that we could ask passengers to stand up, then it all came together as the seat flipped over. It improved the whole experience from dining, to being able to have a single seat that is both a window and an aisle seat.

It all came about because we framed the problem in a different way. We took market share and had an effective ROI as there was less discounting. It also gave the Virgin Atlantic design team great kudos. Plus we licensed the patent for the design and made extra licensing income from other businesses that wanted to use the seat.

Joe Ferry, Former Head of Design, Virgin Atlantic

Case example: Assumptions constraining innovation at ITV

There is an unbelievable amount of sway that an assumption can have – 'we can't do this because of x' – when it's not actually fact. Too many things are stopped or constrained for no reason at all. For example, we launched the ITV Player back in 2007, for which we were buying TV shows like *Gossip Girl* which had to be protected by DRM. The problem was that back then, Windows Media Player was the only real DRM solution. The Windows Media Player was a real pain as users needed the right version and they had to download the correct key. It was a real hassle for them and around 50% of people failed to view content just because of DRM issues.

We kept going for a year and then I went into a meeting with the senior executives and asked to change the rights so that they would be DRM free, as it was killing the business. The key stakeholder then asked, 'Are we sure it is a requirement?' when I thought he was the one who had said it was a requirement in the first place. So we dropped all DRM for ITV and others soon followed.

Richard Harding, Former Director of Technology, ITVonline, ITV

Visualise early

Creating a common understanding of the proposition is critical to success and when delivered through written reports and PowerPoint presentations, it can be hard to do. Creating a mock-up of the proposition as early as possible can provide a wealth of benefits. First, it helps communicate the proposition to stakeholders, who will normally be far more able to quickly understand a picture of the solution rather than a report describing it. It can also help work through some of the detail on how the experience and processes will actually work. In this way, stakeholders from operations, regulation and legal can get a far quicker understanding of the implications of the proposition. Finally, a visualisation can be the best form of soliciting feedback from customers, particularly if you are able to turn the visualisation into a working prototype that enables testing of the full customer experience.

During the early stages, the proposition may still not be developed enough to create a full mock-up, but it is still possible to bring the idea to life with anything from advertising concepts, to cartoon animation or video. Anything to bring it to life and demonstrate the unique selling points of the product or service. These days, mocking up a website or app, and even using 3D printing to produce lifelike prototypes of physical products, are all quick and cost-effective, so there is little excuse for failing to bring a new proposition to life early on in the process.

Case example: Developing support through early visualisation at British Gas

When somebody comes up with a great visual of how to sell it to the customer, it can transform the project. Anybody can do PowerPoint and create a logical story, but when people look at something and go, 'Wow', it transcends the logic of PowerPoint. We had this on Mobile Energy. Right at the beginning we worked with an agency who mocked up the screens on tablets and iPhones. We just made up the brand and mock-ups in less than a week and then went straight to the board. There was no PowerPoint, or business case, but they understood the concept and they loved it.

Sometimes you just get so absorbed in the details and the logic that you lose sight of what the customer is actually getting and the simple big picture view.

Phil Kohler, Proposition Director, British Gas

Case example: Engaging the organisation to speed up delivery of the new Breakfast Experience at Hampton Inn hotels

This was a two-year project that was fraught with challenges. First we had to get stakeholders to understand the need for change. Hampton is a very successful brand and nothing was going wrong and customer satisfaction was good, but I believe that there is no better time to improve and put yourself further in front of the competition. We were already the leader and there is a culture of leadership and wanting to maintain that.

Our fixtures and containers were the same as everybody else's, just off the shelf, but we wanted something different and differentiating. It would need to pass the test of time and be flexible to our changing needs over the next five to ten years. I was inspired by my ten-year-old son's Lego set where he can build anything so we wanted a modular display that is very flexible and interchangeable. It was a highly cross-matrix group of people coming together; vendors, partners, researchers, consultants and we even brought in an aerospace designer. It sounds like overkill, but we nailed it and now everybody across our 2000 hotels will be required to be retrofitted.

You have to get lots of engagement at the beginning. That way you get the challenges early and get everything on the table. Sometimes you just have to listen and acknowledge and then will get buy-in. Listen – don't talk. But it can't be done by consensus, otherwise it gets watered down to vanilla flavour.

You have to understand the glacial pace that innovation comes at in large organizations. It is painful for those of us working in it. You have to be patient to get your mind around the timeframes your organization moves at.

Otherwise it becomes frustrating and you'll fall out. It's like the ocean – you can't change it but have to learn to navigate it.

We could have gone faster. I think if we'd had more reality checks and brought the people who had to operationalize it in earlier. Also visualizing it. Everybody who saw it on paper hated it. They just couldn't get their minds around it, but as soon as they saw proper designs and non-production samples, they loved it. We could have done that earlier to get buy-in quicker.

Mark Southern, Director, Product Innovation – Food & Beverage, Hilton Worldwide

b

There is a risk of over-promising to stakeholders by creating realistic prototypes. Stakeholders often see a demonstration and don't understand that it isn't connected to any real systems or data and that it will actually take months or even years to deliver. Whilst frustrating, this friction is actually a positive one as it creates a greater sense of urgency and belief in the project. Nevertheless, it needs to be managed carefully as there is a danger that the team building the innovation start to become viewed as creating *smoke and mirrors* and failing to deliver.

Customer research into new products and services can be misleading

When developing new products or services, it is common to hear that customer research is the most important thing. It is true that the innovation must address a clear and strong set of customer needs and so it is right that the voice of customer is king.

However, the challenge is how to get meaningful customer insights. There are a whole range of qualitative and quantitative research techniques, including focus groups, interviews, customer diaries, behaviour tracking and quantitative surveys. Yet despite so many methodologies, they all tend to provide overly positive indications and none can reliably answer the key question pertaining to whether the innovation will be strong enough to succeed: will enough customers pay enough money for this product or service?

This is because all of these methodologies suffer from four main issues:

1. **There is far more focus on the product during research than in real life** – Potential customers spend far longer considering a product during research than they would in real life, resulting in very different research responses to how they actually behave in practice. Estimates of how many marketing messages people see per day vary massively from 250 to 20,000, but what is consistent is an understanding that a company has only a few seconds to grab a potential customer's attention and convey their key messages. Some of the above techniques take hours, none of them less than minutes.

2. **Consumers may behave very differently in real life to their perception of a hypothetical question** – People might say they want the best or the cheapest or the fastest product, but in real life they may trade-off speed for cost, or quality for simplicity, and so their behaviour ends up being quite different. The Google search results case study below is a great example of this.

3. **People often say what they think we want to hear** – Focus groups in particular can suffer from significant bias depending on the abilities of the moderator, but in all cases, during research people tend to overstate their likelihood to buy a new product and their level of interest in it.

4. **Most importantly, researchers normally hear what they want to hear** – This starts with the design of the research itself. Often customer research is set up to prove a certain hypothesis and all too often we look for positive affirmation

of a new product's potential and ignore some of the negatives, rather than trying to truly test it. We explain negative feedback away with phrases like, "That was the wrong customer", or "They didn't fully understand." We have too much vested in the project to properly take on board the negative comments and it is always easy to manipulate research feedback, whether quantitative or qualitative, to say what we want to hear, or want an investment committee to hear. Yes, we may make some tweaks to the offering but rarely will somebody in the team put their hand up and say "Actually, this project that we've all been working on for nine months just isn't going to work."

b

Case example: Consumers saying one thing and doing another at British Airways

Airport lounges are a hygiene factor for premium airlines but it's really hard to prove they have any incremental value in a business case. So we ended up having a tiered approach, categorising lounges by importance and commercial value with our two full spec flagship ones at JFK and Heathrow, then BA branded lounges at around 30 focus cities and use of third-party lounges in less profitable stations. This allowed us to differentiate where appropriate whilst managing costs. We included pre-flight dining in key airports as research showed that passengers wanted to just sleep on shorter routes (e.g. JFK to London) – but the truth was that many ended up eating both in the lounge and in the air. It's the same with what they eat, passengers often say they want healthy food, but the less healthy options are always more popular.

Emily Clark, Former Product Development Manager, British Airways

Customer research obviously has a strong role to play, but there is no reliable way of researching the commercial potential of projects without actually testing them with live customers. For all of these reasons, research can be dangerous as it creates a false sense of security amongst the project team and stakeholders alike.

In this way, average and sometimes even poor ideas pass through stage-gates, whilst good ideas fail to be improved into great ones. This is often blamed on the research, yet the real fault lies in our over-reliance on customer research in the first place and at the same time on our own natural response of only hearing what we want to.

However, just because it needs to be treated with caution, does not mean that it is worthless and should be ignored altogether. Some people have great gut instinct, but few of us can bring that to bear on every project, and research still has a valuable role to play, as shown in the Pfizer example below.

Case example: Ignore research at your peril at Warner-Lambert

The Marketing VP believed that consumers wanted a strong chewing gum, that there was a niche market for a strong non-sweet, even bitter taste. The market research didn't support that – it showed consumers wanted a sweet taste. His gut feel overruled and so R&D developed it. It ran in a simulated test market and did poorly, but again the argument was that it was only a simulated test market which didn't prove anything and so it was put on the market. It bombed. This all came from one individual following his gut rather than being objective and listening to the research.

Some people believe that they know better than research, that customers don't know what they want until you give it to them. This is true in some cases, but usually if the evidence says no then it is no. It's usually best to give customers what they say they want rather than what they say they don't want and there is a big difference between customers not knowing what they want and knowing what they don't want…

Arthur Fox, Former Global Director Consumer Insights and New Products Identification, Pfizer Consumer Healthcare

In some instances customer research can give false negatives. For example, if you had asked customers 20 years ago whether they would pay for bottled water or packs of pre-chopped lettuce, you would have received some pretty negative responses, yet according to the Beverage Marketing Corporation the bottled water market has grown by well over 50% in the last ten years, and these two markets alone are worth billions today.

Customer research programmes can also become tired, with similar needs and trends appearing from multiple studies. This drives researchers to try new methodologies and techniques, or try a broader perspective of customers such as your customer's customer in a B2B context or the customer's family in B2C context. These can help give new perspectives and insights as long as researchers and innovators are still alive to the caveats above.

b

Case example: Customers act differently to the preference they state in research at Google

For a while the number of Google search results displayed on a page was ten simply because our founders thought that was the best number. We eventually did a test, asking users, 'Would you like 10, 20 or 30 search results on one page?' They unanimously said they wanted 30. But ten results did far better in actual user tests, because the page loaded faster. It turns out that providing 30 results was 20% slower than providing ten, and what users really wanted was speed. That's the beautiful thing about data – it can either back up your instincts or prove them totally wrong.

Susan Wojcicki, Senior Vice President of Advertising, Google

Case example: Misleading consumer research at Yum Brands

At Yum Brands, we decided to create a natural pizza for the Pizza Hut brand. Intuitively, nobody wants a pizza that's better for you. But this experience was consumer driven rather than internal, and we got consumers in to build it with us, hands on with the chefs.

There was lots of push back at first from the organization but we managed to win the franchisees round by:

- Showing them the consumer data (e.g. McDonalds was moving into salads and grilled chicken)

- Tasting in the lab early changed their perceptions of the product and enabled them to feed in to it and make them feel like they are part of it

- Creating a test market with two of the most vocal franchises to get them on board as advocates

So we got it launched, but nine months later it wasn't in the stores anymore because consumers didn't buy it. Despite it being a great innovation, done in the right way, at the end of the day consumers weren't prepared to make the trade-off. They were going to have their normal indulgent pizza on a Saturday night and then come Monday they'd eat a healthy meal to lessen their guilt of indulging with pizza.

Shannon Bryan, Former Marketing Director, Pizza Hut

Test and learn early

Rather than asking customers in research whether they like certain features and designs of our offerings, and how many of them are likely to buy it, all of which are susceptible to the problems above, we should simply test the solution for real to prove whether customers actually will buy this product or use that feature. That means charging full price for an early prototype product as per the MVP approach and seeing the reality of whether the project can survive.

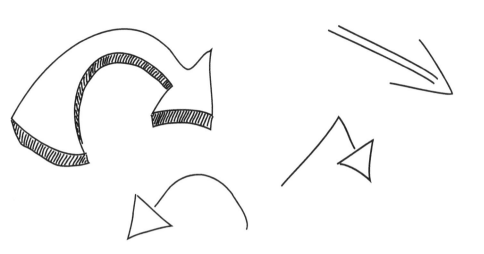

"You can't learn from **PowerPoint."**

Different marketing and sales channels and price points can all be tested, for example on a regional basis, but all with the purpose of proving, or disproving, a sustainable commercial model. Products can still be iterated and improved and those early customers rewarded with new versions or other benefits. In this way, we are truly understanding the potential and getting real feedback.

There are often opportunities to test new products and services on a small scale, and sometimes this can even create additional buzz and attraction. For example, it is common for Fast Moving Consumer Goods (FMCG – or CPG for American readers) manufacturers to test a new product by selling it as a limited edition. This means that if it doesn't work out then withdrawing it is not seen as a failure, which of course it is not as it is merely testing the market. It can also be used to create additional buzz and excitement around the product to give it the best chance of success. Hence this being a limited edition book.

"You need to be learning from trials. That's why chocolate manufacturers keep launching these limited editions – it's a great way of trying new stuff at small scale."

Meldrum Duncan, Co-Founder, Curious Industry

This principle of testing a product before a full launch is not restricted to chocolate bars and books – pop-up stores can be used for a wide range of products to create a short-term channel that doesn't impact standard channels. Also, festivals, events and promotions can be used to create a fixed period of time to test new offers and still have the same effect.

Prototypes need to be built early, but not without proper consideration. The first stage of prototype emerges from the early visualisations highlighted above. It is important to explore the full end-to-end experience and have a strong understanding of the core proposition before attempting to build a full working prototype, as time and resource can easily be wasted if there is a lack of clarity.

The best way of achieving this clarity is some form of *paper prototyping* – walking though the full experience and feature set to understand what happens at each step of the process and how to create an experience that reflects the vision of the proposition and addresses the customer problem. These paper prototyping exercises are most effective when combining the designers or engineers who will build the prototype, together with the business and operations people who fully understand the way processes currently work and customer behaviour, and of course the core team building the new proposition.

b

Case example: Learning with real customers at Powershop

Most large organisations are commercially focused and, to manage risk, are compelled to analyse the hell out of everything before doing anything. This requires so much evidence that they can be paralysed for quite some time whilst looking for the perfect answer.

We took a slightly more risky but ultimately better approach. If you've got a hunch that's counter to the norm, in our case that customers might actually enjoying knowing more about their energy usage, you need to prove it in the real world. You can't get confidence from desk analysis. We needed real live customers.

No amount of preparation gets you ready for that first customer. And once you've got the first, you can get the second. Once you have a few, they'll help you get a whole lot more. Customer satisfaction creates more customers. It's the only way to do it. Naturally, corporate parents want the confidence that you know what you're doing and a good business plan does that. We had an outrageously optimistic plan but that inspired confidence. It's hard to start something without imagining you're going to do incredibly well.

We were fluid and made rapid changes, even on the day. We were not really following the agile processes we needed to adopt as we grew, we just did it anyway. There were only a handful of people making decisions about how the offering would evolve. We had to understand our positioning and pricing strategy and execute this really well. We sought insight from mentors and experts to determine good pricing practice and customer experience and when the two came together it made for a killer combination. We launched with a great customer experience at the lowest price in the market. That really helped us get off the ground.

Simon Coley, Creative Director, Powershop

Case example: Trialling outside of core systems at ATB Financial

At ATB, we have a great core banking system, but we keep coming up with crazy ideas and business models that require quite a lot of change and the core IT team struggle to cope with small prototypes and we're not even on the radar in terms of priorities. So we work with small, nimble third parties. For example, on a crowdfunding project, we worked with a small shop that created a platform and then there's a new savings proposition, which is really core to our business, but we still couldn't get resource to do a pilot. So we worked with a local app development company and a payments company and we're now pushing for a sandbox in our budget for next year so that we can prototype easier.

We leverage our employee base to trial and get feedback but try to make it as real as possible – although we're having to build bank accounts outside of our core systems which means not all of the functionality is perfect. But we still do it and soft launch into our customer base. The top executives are really well engaged and they understand that we can't do a business case whilst building pilots, more that pilots inform the business case.

James Gamage, Managing Director of Innovation, ATB Financial

Create momentum

Innovation projects can often become bogged down as the various stakeholder groups, steering boards, decision makers and approval processes take time to give them the green light. Therefore, it is important to establish and maintain energy and momentum around the project.

This can be achieved in part by being good at PR both internally and externally. Innovation is normally a really positive message that people are interested in and publicising milestones and events can be a great way of gaining great perception and building momentum. That said, you have to get to those milestones and events in the first place and one of the most effective ways of doing this is setting frequent, tight deadlines for the project team to be delivering against. This keeps pace in the team and should enable quick decision-making so that the team can pivot quickly as they learn what does and does not work.

Such speed can feel uncomfortable for the team, as there is no time for perfecting anything and little time to overcome the many roadblocks along the way, but as long as the decision makers involved at the deadlines are cognisant of the approach and supportive of the team, then speed is an effective way of keeping the project moving.

Likewise, it is important that these reviews and deadlines are action orientated. There is always a risk that they can become forums for discussion and that the decision makers ask for more detail before progressing. In such an uncertain environment, it is understandable why this might happen, but once the team start answering non-critical questions, or with more detail than is relevant, then the project will slow and grind to a halt. It is important that there is strong leadership and the right decision-making forum to avoid this unnecessary brake on projects.

Case example: Aggressive deadline forcing fast delivery at Air Canada

We created an airline in 11 weeks for Air Canada. We named the new offer Rouge, which was a snappy bilingual name and a radical and distinctive livery, given the culture of the organization. We showed it to the CEO and he just said yes. Driven by an aggressive deadline meant that intuition and instinct played a much bigger role than traditional programs. Normally, those initial, intuitive impulses that drive so much innovation are quelled by the bureaucratic processes associated with corporate decision-making – you're not allowed to trust your gut, but our deadline in this particular circumstance meant that we just had to go for it. We just went with our hearts because we had to paint the plane in a couple of months. There was no time for collective bargaining. Luckily we had an efficient line to the top. It can be easy to make things complicated and cluttered but this didn't allow for that.

Paul Wylde, Founder and Creative Director, PaulWylde

Do not become emotionally wedded to the proposition

Having just stated the importance of momentum and how best to achieve this, there is an equally important caveat against becoming over-attached to the proposition and trying to get it delivered at all costs. Sometimes teams can develop bunker mentality, where they start ignoring some of the issues with the proposition. They just try to launch it, knowing deep down that it does not feel quite right, but after all the effort they have put in they are not prepared to see it fail.

Case example: Too much momentum

We actually set up a new business that was due to go live shortly, and the call centres already had access to the product. Then somebody junior in the team alerted me that he felt the offer wasn't fit for purpose. So I got the team together and asked each one individually for a 'Go' or 'No go' call from their specific work stream perspective. 12 out of the 14 of them said no, yet as a collective, they would have seen it switch on. It was mainly a quality issue, so we delayed it and got it right before hitting the button. It's like the launch of Saturn 5 when the guy checks the fuel and the engines and so on before the launch. Some people worry about what people will think if you pull it, but that is still the right thing to do. You have to remember that.

Peter Haigh, Director, Energy Market Risk

b

Case example: Over-resilience on mobile-phone wallets at O2

We were trying to build a mobile-phone wallet. There was support for the product and most of the senior team who had seen it believed that it would be a good product. Maybe there was some 'group think', and we believed we needed to do it and do it big, but we didn't manage to find a better way of testing it before launch. You can be so much smarter now with test and learn platforms. Before, you just kept going on the hope that it would be OK. There was too much product push, where we were building a product and we would find a way to make it work. The way we researched was inadequate. Now I'd be far more robust and scientific. We got locked into a delivery mindset and how fast we could get it out of the door. So we got it launched but it was not as effective as it could or should have been and took time to get it right.

Tim Sefton, Former Business Development Director, O2

Summary

> ➤ **Idea iteration is generally reactive to barriers and challenges in its way, rather than generating proactive improvements** – Put in place regular reviews to proactively challenge the proposition against the original problem.

> ➤ **Stay true to the proposition without compromise** – Do not let stakeholders water it down.

> ➤ **Challenge all assumptions about the business** – Just because things happen in a certain way, does not mean that they have to happen that way. Challenge these assumptions to find new ways of overcoming issues.

> ➤ **Customer research into new products and services can be misleading** – Customer research is vital, but understand the risks of research approaches. Testing a paid-for minimum viable product with live customers gives a true perspective.

> ➤ **Visualise early** – Bring the idea to life for customers and stakeholders to really understand it.

> ➤ **Create momentum** – Do not let corporate *treacle* take hold. Push for short deadlines and quick decisions.

> ➤ **Do not become emotionally wedded to the proposition** – Accept that sometimes the idea is not right.

8. Business Case

Apply real commercial rigour.

The business case can be one of the most difficult elements of developing a new venture in the corporate environment. Big businesses are used to having robust plans that can be backed with a high degree of confidence in their return on investment. Unfortunately, very rarely do innovation projects come with such robust forecasts or anything more than just a set of assumptions. Some companies continue to insist on having extensive business case exercises carried out, whilst others lose trust in the innovation forecasts and take to less financial metrics for assessing and investing in projects. So how do you manage the business case challenge for innovation projects in large businesses?

Focus on the key financial drivers of the case

It is remarkably easy to manipulate a spreadsheet to allow a business case to tell a certain story. Business case models can easily become overly complex, particularly for businesses that are used to dealing with mature, complex products that are deeply understood, as it provides reassurance that the financials have been properly looked at. However, typically the more complex the model, the easier it is to manipulate as there are more assumptions to adjust and hide. This can lead to confusion over the real levers driving the new product or business and often results in conversations about depreciation rather than sales volumes or other critical elements.

The most important thing is to focus on the big assumptions that have a significant impact on the financial case. Normally, it is obvious which these are, but sensitivity modelling can soon identify the impact of individual assumptions and help understand the top three to five assumptions to focus on. The fact is that whatever the assumptions are, they will almost always be wrong. The important thing from the proposition perspective is to understand them so that the focus for testing is on those assumptions, and adjustments can be made quickly.

Making sure that one of the finance team creates and owns the model can be a big help. Not just because of using their skills and matching the standard formats, but it will also increase the level of trust of the case within the finance community. At the same time, it's still important for the team to own the assumptions and the model itself.

Case example: Dealing with wrong assumptions and over-ambition at O2

I started when giffgaff was just an idea on PowerPoint around collaborating with customers, with a simple and online experience. There was an ambitious business case which made it hard to get the opportunity to evolve as we were just focused on trying to hit numbers.

There were lots of assumptions on the target market which led to some simple pricing assumptions, data was not even in the plan. Lots of research had been done in order to get board sign-off and they'd identified this segment of 'ambitious status seekers' who were 30+, with some money to spend but were shunning the big mass market brands. There was an ambitious social media marketing plan that assumed that word of mouth and viral videos would drive growth with a very low marketing budget. All of these assumptions were wrong except for the underlying idea about the customer community involvement. From day one, the online forum was always busy (I'd feared there might be tumble weed), involvement has been great and we've had super-users staying up all night when we've launched new products to help other customers. The identified segment turned out to be not really bothered enough by their attitudes to change mobile supplier and another segmentation study showed the group we thought we were targeting were actually much older than we thought and less internet savvy and we needed to focus on younger people who wanted better value through bundles.

There was an imperative from the business to get something out quickly and it took 12 months from launch to iterate it into the right place with changes to tariff bundles and payment by vouchers. The online virals were really difficult, both to get to go viral and to convey the right message. We got over 100 videos but the quality wasn't good enough. So our original marketing strategy just didn't work.

The good thing was that Telefonica gave us the freedom to do it – to act like a start-up, recruit a new team, have a different office, use the bare minimum IT resource from O2 and do the rest ourselves – and this all enabled the pivoting we needed.

The business plan was very ambitious (with payback after 14 months) and was actually unfeasible and unbelievable. Evidence showed the community as popular and we had learnt about the segment we were after and had found the right price but we were within one month of being shut-down as we were missing our year one targets by 85%. It was pretty hairy. But we still had enough support to keep it alive past that first year and thereon it became a more normal ride. We've had scaling issues and have been focusing on getting our systems more stable.

Now we're five years into the project, including the first year of design and development, and actually if you remove that first year after launch to allow for pivoting and learning, then the subsequent three years have actually pretty much matched the original business plan targets. It should have just allowed an extra year at the bottom of the hockey stick.

There was over-reliance on the research that was done and no allowance for pivoting in the first 12 months. Research is always wrong as things will always be different from the plan and you need to allow time for them to evolve.

Mike Fairman, CEO, giffgaff

Balance ambition and realism

New projects are always competing for resource and funding. This brings pressure to show large potential revenues or other financial benefits in the business case. Typically, whatever caveats are put around such numbers are soon forgotten, but the number remains, inked in to next year's plan. Suddenly the proposition has a large target to achieve, which can drive entirely the wrong behaviours. If it is understood that there is an important problem to solve for the customer in a strategically important area for the company, with a proposition that is completely untested, then the important thing is to establish the proposition in the market, learn what works and what does not, and invest for growth once it is right. However, an inflated year one target changes the focus to simply being about hitting revenue and profit targets, which can lead to very different and unintended results.

Case example: Inflated revenue targets at BT

The biggest error is to go very public with high ambitions too early.

The chairman announced that BT were going to grow the top-line by 8% and suddenly there was lots of excitement around the growth ventures which we hadn't even launched yet. Suddenly there was huge pressure for growth. Soon after the launch of BT Click&buy we got some good content partners on board and hit 1,000 transactions in a day. This felt like a good threshold so I sent a message to my boss… who forwarded it to his boss… who forwarded it to the CEO who called me and asked how much revenue that was worth. I still remember the silence at the end of the phone when I told him that we only made a small commission off each transaction and that I probably had more money in my wallet than we'd made off the transactions.

We did the business case for BT Click&buy and at the start we showed the gross transaction value as top-line revenue. The finance team highlighted that we could only count the 20% commission on that transaction value as revenue. To get over this problem, they just multiplied our target by five to keep the top-line target the same. It was absurd and it has happened everywhere I've gone. They give you a target which is totally unrealistic and then you negotiate down from bonkers to unachievable and it puts you on the back foot from day one. You're chasing revenue and defending yourself rather than focusing on the overall business.

Often these business cases are inflated to get support, when fundamentally they just aren't good enough to merit investment and shouldn't get signed off.

Ian Price, Former CEO, BT Click&buy

It is important to return to the original purpose of the proposition, which may be about growing market share, or accessing a new customer segment, or defending a competitive threat. These objectives may not lead to significant short-term revenue growth and the model needs to reflect the real purpose rather than suddenly turn into a new profit centre as soon as a stakeholder challenges the business case.

It's not just year one either. New venture or product business cases are notorious for showing a hockey stick growth curve, with strong and straight revenue growth once up and running. There are two main issues with this:

> ➤ **Three-to-five year forecasting** – Whilst it's normally important to know that the product has potential to reach a certain scale and be profitable, it's hard enough to forecast revenues for the first year or 18 months. Trying to forecast them for three or in some cases even five years is not sensible.

> ➤ **Allowing for plateaus** – As we know, not every new proposition takes off, but when they do it's incredibly rare for them to grow in a straight or even exponential line. The reason for this is that rarely are they built for significant

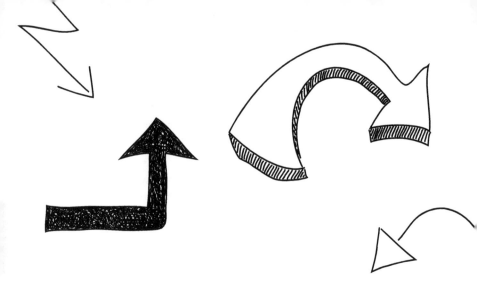

" An inflated year one target changes the **focus to simply being about** hitting revenue and profit targets, **which can lead to very different** and unintended results. **"**

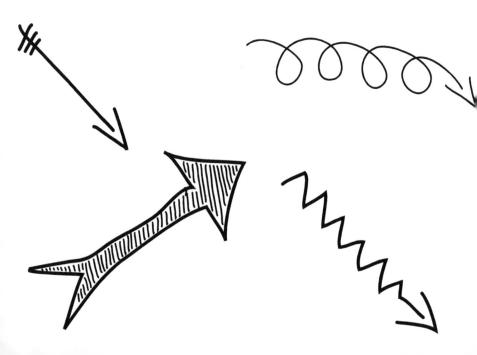

scale at launch – and rightly so. Therefore, as growth takes off, they need to build more robust delivery mechanisms – be it call centres, production lines, logistics, or IT platforms. This requires investment not just of money but of time and focus, and these together with the inevitable teething troubles of changing any of these processes will invariably lead to bumps in growth. Therefore, if you are modelling for growth, be sure to model in the slower growth and plateaus associated with investing in scaling.

Look for alternative commercial solutions

One of the most common barriers faced by innovation teams is getting the business case for a project to meet internal financial hurdles. These often include limits on payback, breakeven or internal rate of return (IRR). This is understandable from the business perspective as it needs a standard way of comparing, managing and prioritising different projects across the company from a commercial point of view. However, given how much projects tend to evolve leading up to launch and then post-launch, and the uncertainty surrounding any financial projections for a new venture, spending time detailing future profitability makes little sense.

It is a waste of time for the innovation team to focus on manipulating a business case so that it meets the desired hurdles, rather than focusing on making sure that the basic fundamentals stack up. The team will often be massaging numbers that have been made up anyway, and it can lead to too much emphasis being placed on individual assumptions in the business case rather than the fundamentals of the project.

Nevertheless, these hurdles always exist in one form or another and teams need to be able to find the best way of commercialising any given project. This is rarely delivered by adjusting a take-up figure or a cost assumption on a spreadsheet in the hope that everything will be OK, but more by looking at alternative business models or investment strategies that will match the venture to the underlying objectives and constraints of the wider business.

Sometimes, even if a project meets these standard financial requirements, it still may not get approval if it is not as strong as another project or simply just too small to be meaningful or, most commonly, there is not the appetite to invest significant sums in risky ventures. However, there are ways of combating these challenges, and the innovation team need to find ways of making the investment more palatable, as in the examples below.

Case example: Commercial hurdles forcing innovative design at British Airways

The existing Club World seat was old and tired and customers were crying out for the ability to sleep on long flights. As most of the profit for premium airlines is in the business class cabin, we couldn't afford to lose out to competitors in this key market. As the new design enabled the seat to turn into a flat bed, it occupied a larger footprint on the aircraft, which presented the challenge of optimising the cabin space whilst maximising the number of seats. After evaluating a number of design concepts, as well as hundreds of layouts to reach the optimal configuration, we finally reached a solution that satisfied the needs of both the customer and the business – forwards and backwards facing seats that run head to toe. The other challenge was managing the ergonomic effects of rearward facing flight, which to this day is still a very unorthodox seating position but inherently safer.

Emily Clark, Former Product Development Manager, British Airways

Case example: Commercial hurdles creating success at Tesco

Our team managed revenue generation from non-core areas of Tesco, from vending machines to car washing. When visiting a number of our petrol forecourts to look for new opportunities we noticed that many of the air and water machines were out of service. Back at the office, we found that this was indeed a common issue; it seemed that as they were a free extra service, they were low on the priority list for the maintenance teams. Further digging revealed that this problem was also a cause of around 10% of customer complaints at the petrol stations.

Having worked through some ideas, we trialled a paid for service at three sites, whereby customers would pay 20p for access to the air pump. With revenue associated with the machines we'd be able to increase profit and the machines would be better maintained. This trial was successful with high usage of the machines at the three sites and no complaints.

However, the business was not prepared to invest in hundreds of new air and water machines with payment mechanisms. Whilst it was a reasonable business case, there were simply bigger fish to fry.

Back to the drawing board. One of the team came up with an excellent commercial approach to this problem. We auctioned off the rights to the air and water machines, whereby a supplier would install and maintain the machine at their expense in exchange for which they could take a percentage of the revenue it generated. We retained the remaining percentage and they paid us for using our sites through the upfront auction. Due to the revenue share, the supplier was naturally incentivised to keep the machines up and running. The scheme took off. The complaints dropped to insignificant levels, we'd saved our maintenance teams a headache, customer satisfaction at the petrol forecourts actually increased, a small supplier had a big growth opportunity and, without investing a penny beyond supplier management, we'd generated millions per annum of new revenue that went straight to the bottom line.

Dan Taylor, Former Category Manager Revenue Generation, Tesco

Challenge the business model for new innovations

Typically, teams either follow what the company already knows, such as a wholesale model, or follow what the teams normally do as consumers, and so adopt some form of retailer model. This fails to consider all of the different types fully or where the value is in the supply chain, as there may well be other roles such as manufacturer, white-labeller, aggregator, financer, or broker that may provide significant opportunities for growth and profitability.

Likewise, it is important to consider other revenue models such as Pay as You Go or Contract, Freemium or Premium, commission, franchising, and bundling opportunities.

Understanding sources of value and how best to access them can turn an average business case into a very attractive one.

Case example: Global technology firm licensing IP to reduce risk

We were reviewing a set of new non-invasive medical monitoring technologies that our client had acquired the rights to. These were able to take heartbeat, blood pressure and blood sugar readings from a simple watch-style monitor and could be of significant potential in the fitness and healthcare markets.

However on review, all of the technologies had some issues that needed further development, whether it was cost or reliability, which meant there was no obvious 'slam-dunk' or mass-market proposition, although some niche markets looked feasible. We looked at a whole raft of ideas to commercialise the technologies but all of the propositions and ventures looked risky compared to some of the other projects in the portfolio. Whilst this meant the client wasn't prepared to invest further in these technologies at that time, neither did they want to ignore the potential of these exciting technologies. Therefore, we looked for other companies that might be interested in them and starting with a premium fitness company in Canada the client licensed the technology to them.

The result was that the client was able to generate revenues from the technology and enable the continued development of the technologies themselves, whilst at the same time they continued to hold the rights to IP and commercialisation in other markets should the technology take off.

Dan Taylor, Managing Director North America, Market Gravity

Case example: Commercial business model innovation at O2

b

When we built O2 Wifi, which is still doing well with lots of hotspots, it came through the insight of our commercial finance guy. He saw the opportunity to create a new business model. BT were busy building Openzone whose model was to charge customers for the product, but we sold the product to premises and together with them offered it free to consumers – which drove footfall for the premises. We really only did this because we were trying to make our model work – the customer insight came second, but it worked.

Tim Sefton, Former Business Development Director, O2

Think like a start-up

Just as the intention is to encourage start-up behaviour by removing many of the corporate barriers to the proposition, so too should the finance approach be to encourage start-up behaviour.

Primarily, this means moving towards small and frequent funding rounds at the early stages, rather than large annual budgets being handed to project teams, which often happens with more standard, and more predictable, projects. This has the benefit of helping the business manage risk and keep more in control of the investment, and also encouraging the venture team to focus on key metrics and earn the next round of funding.

Case example: Decision tree analysis to communicate and manage investment risk

We had been developing a new venture that would represent a substantial investment for the board. Strategically, there was a strong appetite for the project, but equally there was concern about the level of investment required on what was a risky venture. We carried out the usual work to reassure the decision makers; we dug into every assumption in the business case with a thorough sensitivity and scenario analysis, we successfully trialled the project on a small scale, we carried out substantial customer research, but the FD was still not comfortable enough to sign off the project.

We had a long conversation to get to the bottom of his discomfort, a sentiment which was shared by other board members, and it came down to the size of the investment over the next 12 months to get the business fully up and running and then supporting it through to profitability over a further 18-24 months. There was no way of reducing the investment without compromising the venture, but nevertheless we managed to alleviate the board's concerns.

We re-cut the project plan into distinct phases and allocated the investment requirement to each phase. These phases were then mapped on to a decision tree which showed the level of investment for each phase. In this way, the FD and board were able to see a smaller set of commitments rather than one big one, but also the consequences to potential NPV subject to their decision to say yes or no at any of the decision points. In this way, the board was appeased and, over time, the full investment signed off, and the venture successfully launched and grown.

Dan Taylor, Managing Director North America, Market Gravity

Finally, budget cycles can also be the enemy of innovation. Typically, big businesses set their budgets once a year and if an innovation project appears it may well have to wait until the next annual budget round before getting the funding to move forwards. For this reason, it is important to have a small fund set aside each year to push through innovation projects at the right pace.

Summary

> **Focus on the key financial drivers of the case** – Do not get lost in elaborate spreadsheets. Build a simple model and understand the key drivers to focus your testing on.

> **Balance ambition and realism** – Resist the challenge to set over-ambitious financial targets as these will often drive the wrong behaviours. Rather, link the targets to the underlying objective and to testing and learning.

> **Look for alternative commercial solutions** – Hurdle rates are useful to challenge the thinking about the commercial model. Use them as such rather than a reason to fiddle with Excel spreadsheets.

> **Challenge the business model for new innovations** – Do not just assume that the obvious business model is right. Look at all of the different possible roles and ways of capturing value.

> **Think like a start-up** – Work with frequent, small funding rounds to encourage a start-up mindset.

"Everybody thinks they have
big ideas,
but rarely do they understand
what it takes to actually
make it happen. **"**

Nancy Shea, VP
Global Innovation and
Marketing, Ashland

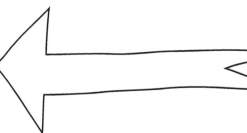

9. Development and Launch

Identify a go-to-market strategy based on the corporate reality as well as the start-up mentality.

Challenge the channel to market early

The importance of creating visualisations and prototypes is highlighted in chapter 7 – these are great ways of really understanding the proposition and communicating it. However, it is increasingly common to see teams overly focus on this front end and spend insufficient time understanding the operations and processes that support it. This is less of an issue with some digital propositions or very incremental opportunities, but anything beyond that needs more. It is a case of building a business, not just a proposition, and understanding the operations plan as well as the marketing plan.

One of the biggest issues is how to sell and service a new offering alongside the core activities of the business. Indeed, one of the most common reasons why new propositions struggle is due to an assumption that it can be successfully sold through existing channels. The theory is that the business already has massive access to the market with a large customer base, strong brand and a range of sales and marketing channels, and all that is needed is to push the new proposition down those channels. Unfortunately, it is rarely this simple, especially if the proposition is anything beyond the incremental.

The sales teams may struggle with new propositions and technologies, systems may need to change, and most commonly the sales channel objectives are not aligned. Typically, the channels will be focused on maximising sales of the most profitable products and services in the business, and so a request to substitute that focus or add on additional targets to try to sell a new, unknown proposition is not normally welcomed unequivocally.

Case example: Trying to borrow core channels at RWE npower

At RWE npower, we set up an energy services venture, now called HomeTeam. The business case was prescribed on leveraging the core channels so we would access the incumbent customer base and cross-sell energy services through the core channels. We did set up our own call centre which worked well, but all the core channels failed to deliver much in the way of boiler care or installations. Effectively you're stealing somebody else's P&L. The Sales Director just wants to sell the products that drive his P&L. This needs alignment of incentives at a high level but that's really hard to do. It's the biggest wrong assumption that most companies make and the funny thing is that normally nobody challenges it until it gets into the field and suddenly it falls over.

Gideon Hyde, Co-Founder & Partner, Market Gravity

Therefore, it is often best to challenge the approach to channels early on when first considering the idea, as often using separate channels to the core business can be more effective, quicker, and provide greater control and ability to test different approaches.

Also, new channels are emerging that can create opportunity in themselves. The expanded reach afforded by an open API approach has already been explained in Chapter 4, but social media is another emerging channel that some companies successfully pursue, as the example below from Cancer Research UK illustrates.

Case example: Social Media driving new donations for Cancer Research UK

Most people on social media just want to chat with friends, and some might talk about good causes, but few want to talk about products or services. Cancer Research UK has a small team of social media managers on a round-the-clock rota. One night someone posted a 'no-make-up selfie', presumably in response to selfies from the Oscars, and within a few hours someone had done one saying theirs was for breast cancer. Overnight, one of the social media managers spotted this and the team joined the conversation and they did it with a supportive comment and their own no-make-up selfie but holding a placard saying 'text beat cancer at ### to donate a few pounds'. Within five days of that first post, nearly 3 million people had donated £8m. This was a great example of leveraging social media.

So many companies are missing the point on social media. You can't create a social media platform – you need to take user-generated content and steer it.

Tim Thorne, Former Innovation Director, Cancer Research UK

Just as you should stop and pause before trying to use the core channels for sales and marketing of new propositions, so too with the servicing of it. For many of the same reasons, including the extra training and likely mismatch with targets, it can make sense to either ring-fence a separate team to deal with customer service on new propositions or find an alternative way of delivering the right experience.

Case example: Creating an end-to-end experience at British Gas

Mobile Energy was a great project because we went back to first principles; looking at the target segment, their needs, and how to differentiate and so on. Then we built an end-to-end proposition around that. The biggest challenge was getting everything aligned so that the proposition is consistent with the entire experience.

Often when you launch a proposition, it's really just an offer, and you don't make too many changes to what goes on behind the scenes, so you just rely on the normal business working, whether that's billing, the call centre, or debt collection. The problem comes when you have a new proposition that needs a different experience. We found that a great way of getting round this problem was making the app the primary touch point. That gave us full control of the entire experience. We had to ring-fence a call centre team and train them differently too and create the whole process – we actually cleaned up a lot of things as we went.

Sometimes, no matter how great the proposition is, a business process hits the customers at some point and it falls over, so you have to design a different answer outside of the normal way of doing things.

Phil Kohler, Proposition Director, British Gas

The difficulty of acquiring and leveraging new capabilities

Many corporates underestimate which new capabilities are needed and how hard these are to develop when launching new ventures. It is common at the early stages of an idea for there to be a buzz because of the capabilities a corporate has to launch a new venture, whether it is its brand, or channel to market, or operational capabilities. These may even become part of the rationale to go ahead with the project, one of the unique selling points. Indeed, some ventures are built purely on this concept, such as Caterpillar building a successful footwear and clothing range around its brand image.

Yet it is just as common that at the same time as highlighting these great capabilities, any missing capabilities are ignored until the implementation stage of a project. For some of these capability gaps, a simple procurement process and commercial contract can deliver a reliable supplier. However, for those capabilities which are seen as core to the venture, and hence will need to be tightly controlled, the problem can be far more challenging.

Broadly, there are three normal routes to resolving this challenge:

b

Delivering Innovation Projects

1. **Build** – Creating capability from scratch is always a slow process as teams have to be recruited individual by individual and then all of the required processes and technologies developed and iterated from a blank piece of paper.

2. **Partner** – Bringing in an expert partner is the quickest and easiest short-term solution, but reduces control and increases bureaucracy and may still be an imperfect solution.

3. **Acquire/invest** – Acquiring a small business that already has the capability seems attractive, but the reality is normally that it is only attractive to the small business, which suddenly has cash and a strong order book, whereas the corporate ends up trying to manage a small business which is unlikely to be perfect. Lots of good things about that small business will be lost by the takeover or investment as the corporate is not trying to make the business the best it can be, but just solve an internal capability gap. Corporates, certainly in this situation, are not venture capitalists and should not consider themselves as such.

Figure 3.1 (see page 52) provides a guide to approaching this dilemma as trying to do everything internally can overstretch any team. Everything from using external consultants or contractors, to partnering with other organisations, can be important tools in bringing in additional skills and the manpower necessary to enable a successful launch. Partners can sometimes bring other less expected benefits too, such as in the British Gas example below.

Case example: Range of benefits of partnering at British Gas

We were launching a new smart homes product and needed to provide a call centre support function for customers. Whilst our core business had a significant call centre operation that was perfectly capable of coping with account and billing queries, they would not be able to handle calls of a technical nature. Establishing a technical centre would take significant time and cost, as these wouldn't be standard customer service representatives but technically qualified staff. Also, given the stage of the project, scale requirements were uncertain, ranging from hundreds of staff if it took off, to just a handful if sales took a slower trajectory and technical calls were less common than assumed. Based on this reasoning, and the non-core nature of the service, we contracted an external supplier to handle this technical service.

The supplier was small in itself, so keen and flexible, but part of a much larger retail conglomerate that made it stable. The technical service provided went well, but there were a number of additional benefits that emerged as our relationship with the supplier grew. First, the technical service team, having become familiar with the product, became important advocates who spread word about the service to the hundreds of people they dealt with every week – not just our customers. As a group of expert users, they were often the first to suggest new practical ideas to improve the product, and finally the supplier became an important channel as we first introduced a promotion for all their employees across the conglomerate and then extended this to a public proposition through some of its standard retail channels. A simple technical service contract had brought in both product improvements and new customers as well as the service they were contracted to provide.

Dan Taylor, Former Director of Innovation, British Gas Smart Homes

Ensure brand development has a halo effect on the corporate as well as supporting the new proposition

For many new products branding is not a big issue. Yet in some cases – and often when entering new markets – it can be seriously underestimated. On the one hand, the parent brand can be constraining and convey the wrong values for some propositions, whereas on the other hand it can be a massive asset which brings high awareness and an identity that customers will understand. Within this context, there are three broad options for branding of new propositions and ventures:

1. **Parent brand** – Use the existing parent brand.

2. **New brand** – Create an entirely new brand.

3. **Sub-brand** – A hybrid approach that creates a new brand supported by the parent brand.

Where new products fit within the core portfolio, it is a relatively simple task to create a product name and design within the parent brand. However, just because a product is outside of the standard range it does not mean it needs new or different branding. If the attributes of the parent brand are relevant and customers can understand the link then the parent brand can be appropriate, as shown in the BT Baby Monitor example below.

b

Case example: Using the core brand to launch Baby Monitors at BT

BT Baby Monitors are still out there doing tens of millions of revenue every year and they are one of the market leaders. It came from a gadgets project which was based around themes. One of the themes was targeting the health sector. We looked at what health means and where BT had the right to play. It turned out that it was not NHS contracts, but rather that

DECT technology was a key capability and the baby monitor market was a really important issue. The technology was better than Tomy and cheaper than the Philips high-end solution, which were the two market leaders. The market was so polarized that we took the mid-price point between the two and were able to own the mid-market. The technology meant consumers were not surprised by BT doing it, and if anything the brand created real trust that this was a technically strong solution.

Tim Thorne, Former CEO, Edengene

However, sometimes branding does need to be carefully considered, either when companies are deliberately trying to step away from the parent brand, such as when Prudential launched Egg, or the earlier example of Air Canada launching Rouge, or more commonly when companies are trying to enter new markets with new products, where the parent brand holds little relevance and will not easily stretch.

In these instances, companies can either look to develop completely new brands or a sub-brand. Entirely new brands such as Prudential's Egg can require significant investment. The task involves creating awareness and recognition with the target customers, as well as a level of trust to actually purchase from a new brand, as well as the obvious need for the customers to understand the product and why they should buy it. However, it does provide the opportunity to create a fresh brand, a new identity, and values that are not associated with the core brand. This can be critical to success for some ventures, such as O2's giffgaff (see case example on page 142).

If done well, this can be successful – with examples such as Egg, or Admiral Insurance launching confused.com – but this approach removes one of the biggest assets that the corporate is bringing to the new proposition and so it is not a decision to be taken lightly.

There is a middle ground, which is to create a sub-brand that is clearly linked and supported by the parent brand. This is common in the FMCG (or CPG to American readers) industry, with examples such as Nestlé KitKat or Cadbury Dairy Milk. These need to be handled with care though, as they lie within the constraints of the parent brand and lack the freedom to create totally new identities.

Selecting which approach to take requires a clear understanding of what the parent brand does and does not stand for and how far it will stretch. When taking the middle ground approach and creating a sub-brand, brands often try to extend beyond their natural space and if there is no halo effect back on to the parent brand from the proposition then it will normally struggle. Where the halo effect works well, new propositions can be the life-blood of more innovative brands, such as in the NRG example (see page 20).

b

Delivering Innovation Projects

Case example: Focusing on the brand halo at GSK

Knowing what your brand stands for, what makes it special and different, is critical when innovating and thinking about how to maximise halo across the brand. An example of this was when we launched Sensodyne Complete Protection in 2013. To ensure this wasn't seen as simply another multi-benefit toothpaste by consumers and retailers, we focused on the fact that if you have sensitive teeth you need to take special care or the problem can become worse, and that this multi-benefit toothpaste was specially designed for that purpose. To maximise halo across all the Sensodyne range, we used a well-established testimonial campaign that was instantly recognisable to consumers as a Sensodyne ad, but through this vehicle introduced the new condition information and product launch news.

Shafik Saba, Former Global Marketing Director, Sensodyne, GSK

At the opposite end of the spectrum to the halo effect, sometimes new propositions can even have a detrimental impact on the parent, such as in the Philips example below.

Case example: New proposition branding impacting the core brand at Philips

Philips identified an opportunity that the lucrative porn market was growing more mainstream in the UK. There was some insight that led to a proposition for married couples who wanted to be more experimental but weren't going to go into a sex shop, but they would buy it from a high street retailer such as Boots. So we came up with a great product that got good press and some of the big retailers were going to take it.

However, it turned out our healthcare team were pitching a big contract to a US hospital that was run by a fairly religious board. They got wind of the idea and it nearly derailed the contract. On the basis of this the product was pulled. Interestingly, Durex now have launched into this space. We had exactly the same thing happen with a men's grooming product too that was flying off the shelves in the UK, but the US healthcare customers were worried about our corporate focus and the brand stretch. So again, it was pulled.

Georgina Schiffers, Former General Manager, Active Play, Philips

Branding can be an even greater challenge when there is a physical product that requires design, and the design itself may need to reinforce the differentiation. Indeed, the design may even be critical to the differentiation, as so often demonstrated by Dyson. Perceptions of the look and feel of new hardware is an incredibly subjective thing, and trying to align multiple stakeholders around a design can be difficult. It is important to tease out design principles early to avoid a constant iteration of designs based on subjective views.

Case example: Differentiation by design at GSK and Ford

When I launched Sensodyne Complete Protection in 2013, I knew the product idea was a good one but not highly differentiated, there were many other multi-benefit toothpastes out there. However there was still an unmet consumer need, and we had a great new product that met these needs. So we differentiated it through design, and created a simple visual identity that semiotically embodied the benefit of complete protection, but in an ownable asymmetric design, that was used across every consumer touch point, from pack to advertising to in-store experience.

With our visual sense being the most dominant, this approach is unsurprisingly used across categories. When Ford Ka launched back in the mid 1990s, its highly distinctive and polarising styling attracted a disproportionate amount of press and reaction, good and bad. However this was one of the critical factors behind why they didn't need to change the design for over 12 years, it still felt new and different, a great achievement for any car manufacturer who often refresh styling every five years.

Shafik Saba, Former Global Marketing Director, Sensodyne, GSK and Former European Business Strategy Manager

---

Case example: Overcoming subjectivity to expedite the design process at Air Canada

It was interesting as design is subjective, which is really hard to manage with lots of stakeholders with different opinions. Where possible you have to remove the subjectivity and encourage individuals to collectively define a meaningful success criteria – effectively becoming your design strategy. If stakeholders have been heard and if you like, 'designed' the brief, then they are normally supportive ambassadors of the entire process thereafter. People just want to be heard, and interests understood. As long as their concerns are met with empathy, associated processes are normally OK. That's what happened with Air Canada Rouge. There wasn't time to procrastinate, debate or argue, once the initial positioning and design was presented, teams supported and rallied around its development and launch, it was almost as if the new design was a given and not up for debate.

Paul Wylde, Founder and Creative Director, PaulWylde

Understand the detail behind key assumptions

One of the reasons that innovation is so hard is that in addition to dealing in the unknown, you are dealing across every aspect of the organisation. It requires the skill set of a general manager to cover everything from operations to marketing, from sales to the accounting. This need for breadth of perspective is not enough on its own as an understanding of the detail across the new proposition or venture is equally important. Lots of ideas sound good at first and sometimes they can even progress a long way down the development process before some of the real issues emerge. Therefore, it is important to get an understanding of the key assumptions and the detail behind them as soon as possible.

Case example: The devil is in the detail at BOC

Once, we found a £1.5 billion opportunity at BOC and, recognising the potential, put 12 people on it for three months to fast track it. However, within two weeks we realised that the original team had not understood the economics and there was no opportunity there. The board was already excited and we had to let them down gently. The problem had been that it looked attractive from a helicopter view, but so does everything, you have to get into the detail at ground level to understand it. Too high for too long is dangerous and projects can progress too far for too long, when ultimately they are destined to failure. The problem is, nobody looks good when this happens.

Dave Wardle, Former Business Development Manager, BOC Group

Proactively manage the risks that matter

Risk is always a big topic when developing and launching new products and services. As highlighted earlier, if the approach and the culture is right, new projects should be far less risky and there is no need to *be brave*. The reality from a corporate perspective is that there are really only two major risks to worry about:

1. **Brand risk** – It doesn't matter if testing a new product doesn't turn out to be the next $1 billion opportunity. It does matter if that test damages the core brand and the core business starts to lose customers and value because of it.

2. **Investment risk** – It doesn't matter if testing a new product doesn't turn out to be the next $1 billion opportunity as long as the test doesn't cost much. (The *much* being defined by the corporate context.)

These two risks need to be fully assessed before running any market test, and the test must be scoped to minimise these risks. All other risks relate to implementation and can be managed. Sometimes businesses will over complicate risk management, with big spreadsheets listing every risk and mitigation strategy. These spreadsheets tend to take focus away from the two big risks and the handful of main implementation risks, and can instil a false sense of security that everything is under control. Keep focus by not trying to manage more than five risks.

b

Case example: Creating a culture of talking about risk at Ashland

If the culture's wrong, people will be afraid to raise risks and speak openly out of fear of getting shot down. So it is important to engage and train senior management on how to react to new ideas at every stage. It took us about three years to train the teams to talk openly, and explain all of the risks to senior management. Everyone has to trust and respect each other at all stages of innovation so the risks can be dealt with and not turn into major derailing issues of a project. A transparent culture is really important and you need to consistently focus on generating and supporting the right culture for innovative thinking and actions. Now we have the culture where people know that they can speak the truth and that management have your back.

Nancy Shea, VP, Global Marketing & Innovation, Ashland

Sometimes, just because something is new it is perceived as risky. The core business resists the idea of change and points out regulatory, legal or fraud risks in order to maintain the status quo. There are a range of approaches to manage relations with the core business, but one great example of managing both this perception and also the real risks in this area is to follow the approach of Capital One (case example below), which made the fraud department responsible for innovation.

Case example: Corporate risk aversion slowing innovation

When I joined British Gas we launched a helpful app to do easy energy meter readings. We visited customers in their homes and found just how hard meter readings were. Energy meters are in awkward places like at the end of the garden or under the stairs. People needed to submit readings to get accurate energy bills. This is a real hassle and customer reading errors were high. So we created an app and made the dials on the app look exactly like whatever meter that household had. We made it super easy to submit a meter reading. We actually developed a version that took a photo of the meter dials but the risk team stopped it as it would be our fault if the reading was wrong. They wouldn't even allow it if we put a check mechanism in to ask the customer to confirm the reading.

However, now at comparethemarket.com, we're launching something similar. kWh and tariffs are still very difficult to understand and price comparison websites still have forms that are far too long. 84% of UK households have never compared energy costs, according to the

Department of Energy. Our ambition is to help people save money on their expensive energy bills. We want to make it radically simple. So now you can take a picture of your bill with our app and we'll do all the rest. You get a notification of how much you could save and what we've read from your bill. You just need to tap to get the saving and it's all done for you. A totally different experience to British Gas, with a very similar idea.

Benjamin Braun, Associate Director, comparethemarket.com

Case example: Head of fraud as head of innovation at Capital One

I was head of fraud and wanted to disrupt the way we were thinking about it. The results were actually record-breaking but we realised that doing things in the same way wouldn't help us if we wanted to keep breaking records. We were discussing how we could approach things differently, collaborate with more varied groups, bring in more insight, experiment with more creative solutions etc. I didn't realise it at the time but we were talking the language of innovation. So I was asked to form an innovation team as well. Actually the behaviours you need aren't that different. In Fraud you need to do whatever it takes, sometimes in iterative cycles until the job is done.

Another part that's similar is collaboration. Fraud and Marketing departments often have different views and objectives. We are more aligned, we talk early and get involved in the creation of new ideas. That way we can help design things with fraud prevention built in.

Lee Osborne, Innovation & Digital, Capital One

One of the biggest risks to an innovation project is that the project will be killed from above, often for reasons unrelated to the project. It may be that the annual results are below expectations and budgets are cut, or a change of CEO brings a change of focus. Managing short-termism from the core business is discussed in Chapter 12, although the BOC example below provides another approach to managing this risk.

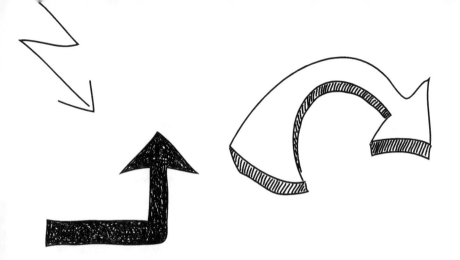

" The CEO has to trust the business owner
and let him run with it.
Don't try to put processes and so on around him.
That is why big companies
find it so hard. **"**

**Michael Johnson, Former
MD New Ventures, Which?**

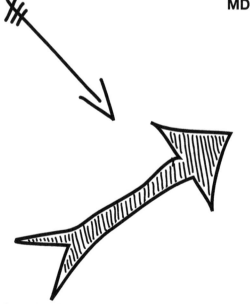

Case example: Managing corporate environment risk at BOC

We ran a big risk workshop and the biggest risk we identified was the board itself – that it would get bored of the programme and cut funding. When we presented back, they were very mature, and guaranteed the funding for five years. A great outcome!

Dave Wardle, Former Business Development Manager, BOC Group

b

Use beta phases to learn and adapt in the live market

Normally, when implementing a new product or service, there will be a series of releases, prototypes or pilots in the market before a soft launch of a live product. This could be anything from friends and family customers who should be more forgiving, to a local or regional trial, or even just a launch but without the marketing campaign, all before the marketing campaign is started for the hard launch. Google is famous for extended beta phases with many of its products staying in beta phase for years, such as Gmail which went live in beta in 2004, and only came officially out of beta five years later when it had over 100 million users.

"GAFA (Google, Apple, Facebook and Amazon) always stand up and announce new products whilst they are still at project stage, certainly well before they are launched. This means that although other brands may get there first, the credit goes to the people who speak about it first."

Benjamin Braun, Associate Director, comparethemarket.com

However, these launches can be dangerous in the politics of a corporate environment. Expectations can immediately change to focusing on sales figures, rather than using them as a real test to improve the proposition before investing heavily in marketing and infrastructure. In fact, these live tests are instrumental and understanding them as experiments rather than soft launches ensures that the focus is on gaining greater understanding to get the product or service right, rather than focusing on driving profit. For these live tests to be successful, it is critical to be able to measure specific elements of the proposition and do so quickly, ideally in real time. However good the proposition, it will need to evolve and you need to know what is working and what is not, and obviously to minimise the time wasted in learning these lessons, so it's fundamental to set up a management information approach and KPIs ahead of going live and to monitor this constantly.

The actual launch for a new product needs careful planning

This series of testing takes much of the risk away from a big launch and reduces the importance of the launch itself. Nevertheless, sometimes a bigger launch is unavoidable, in which case all the aspects of the product launch, be it timing, location, communications and so on, can become more important. It is common to think from the perspective of the new product when is best – for example a gift business might want to launch ahead of the Christmas giving season, or a gym business ahead of the New Year rush – but other considerations such as wider corporate activity, be it core price changes or media attention for whatever reason, can all have an impact, as evidenced by the example below.

Case example: Poor timing and customer communications undermine launch at PG&E

PG&E serves over 5 million customers with gas and electricity in California and was one of the first utilities to rollout smart meters in the USA. Smart meters enable your gas and electricity meter readings to be sent back to the utility automatically, thus generating more accurate bills, better awareness of energy spending and reducing costs of meter reading. Therefore, this was looking at innovation for an electric utility which was new to the world, with new technology and new services.

Our solution was based on a MESH network so we installed the new meters to our customers and then switched them on area by area across the region. Operationally the switch over went very smoothly, but we had a storm of complaints from customers within the first month. It turned out customers' bills had jumped significantly that same month, and they associated it with the new meters, when in fact it was due to a price rise combined with a heatwave that meant everybody had used their air conditioning more than usual. This led to claims of inaccuracy of the meters, and we had to halt the entire programme and get independent auditors to prove their accuracy. But the damage was done, we had people worrying about everything from data privacy and security to fire safety! The fact is we were too late in communicating to customers, even when the benefit seemed obvious to us, and we shouldn't have launched at the same time as a price rise and the heatwave.

Even some of our own employees weren't helpful, and would bad talk the technology to customers. There were lots of people who'd been there for 20 or 30 years without change and suddenly this was new and unknown. It was difficult to know how much training to give them. The core business would still be running for ten years whilst the smart base was growing. You don't go smart overnight. It's a balancing act of employees that are trained. If you don't get that right then the non-believers don't understand the technology. It's not easy and people didn't want to invest ahead of the curve. People weren't malicious, it was just that this was the first real change in their job.

It was the same on the customer side. Our marketing SVP was worried about the haves and the have-nots so didn't want to shout about it right away as millions of customers might be frustrated by having to wait years before they could get a smart meter. So we planned to run silent for a year or two and then go big. Unfortunately, that didn't work. Just enough of the early recipients were dubious about it and we had the high bills issues. We were late on messaging to both customers and employees. Being early is more expensive but worth it.

So you have to get the whole organisation aligned behind a big transformation like that and then get everything from launch timing and communications through to training the frontline staff right, from the start.

Jim Meadows, Smart Meter Project Director, Pacific Gas & Electric (PG&E)

For some ventures, timing can be a fundamental issue, either due to competitor activities as shown in the earlier Virgin Atlantic and British Airways examples and in the 'Unfortunate timing' case example below, but also if the market is not ready for the solution, or the solution is not ready for the market.

Case example: Unfortunate timing

Sometimes you get a 'professional failure' where you have the right skills and team and put a strong plan together but still fail for some reason. I had a project like that with a product targeting a niche segment of the SME market. Five days before our launch, British Gas entered the market with the same thing. It was just bad luck, but we'd been gazumped and had to pull the product – it wasn't a big enough opportunity for the both of us.

Peter Haigh, Director, Energy Market Risk

Case example: Understanding that new innovations have their time at Barclays

We recently opened a new branch in Kensington, that people are excited about and is going well. The thing is that it's almost exactly the same as a pair of branches we opened back in 2000. There are no cashiers, just ATMs for withdrawing and paying in and so on, and then personal bankers. The two previous branches didn't really work and closed in 2003 as they were before their time. Maybe we gave up too quickly and had we stuck at it, we'd already be ahead in this approach.

Likewise, I pushed hard for personalized debit cards. Others had tried this before but it did not take off. That's because it was launched before personal photography had taken off. Now people are really comfortable with the idea of sharing their photos through Facebook and so on. So now personalised cards are a huge success with customers.

So innovation can be going back to something that failed before, if it was the wrong timing. It doesn't always have to be a new idea.

Andrew Harris, Director of Deposits, Barclaycard

b

Invest enough to win

The principles of lean start-up are excellent for developing new products and services more quickly, more cheaply and more effectively. The proposition can be iterated as test and learn cycles direct the evolution of the product, and the customer base will grow as it begins to get traction. However, not all opportunities can just grow linearly from a standing start. Some require a large investment in infrastructure or advertising and it is imperative that corporates give the project the required resources to enable success. Sometimes a venture will prove successful in the trials and require a large investment, but for whatever reason, the corporate chooses to withhold the investment necessary for success – yet still tries to launch on a reduced budget.

This is one area where corporates have a significant advantage over start-ups, not just in their scale, resources, customer base and brand, but they also often have a degree of market power. They can make deals with suppliers that start-ups couldn't possibly negotiate and even influence the shape of the market dynamics through lobbying activity and industry bodies. Leveraging all these advantages can give corporates the edge in the market, if they've made it this far!

Case example: Not investing enough at O2

The broadband market was benign when we started business planning. There was really just BT, Virgin and AOL and they weren't doing much. But as were doing the business case, TalkTalk launched with a free proposition bundled with fixed line (which was subsidising the free broadband). Sky and Orange then both followed suit. All this happened in six months.

To me it was clear that we had to do this properly or not at all. If launching, you should make it a level playing field. Adding fixed line would have cost an extra 25% in capex at a time when our capex budget was frozen. This stopped us doing the fixed line service, so we were consigned to a cheap product (not free) and with no money for marketing so we struggled to get to half a million subscribers whilst Sky flew to 2 million and beyond. By investing bigger, Sky and TalkTalk have become much bigger. In the end we sold it to Sky and got a reasonable ROI, but not the glory it could have been.

Mike Fairman, Former Head of Broadband, O2

Case example: Underselling new innovation at Pfizer

We were working on a children's cough & cold medicine 10 or 15 years ago. These medicines have some bitter tasting active ingredients so it can be a challenge to get children to take them in the traditional forms. Children can't swallow tablets well and liquid medicines and chewables have to taste good. The idea was a frozen popsicle that children could suck. The coolness would sooth the throat and the medicine would be less bitter tasting than the traditional liquid medicines because the popsicle was a larger delivery vehicle for the medicine. We developed and launched it and sold a few million dollar's worth but it never took off. Maybe it was ahead of its time, as now you see a lot more focus in this market with good tasting strips that dissolve in your mouth, and gums and chews that are similar. But perhaps we could have made some different marketing decisions which might have changed the outcome. We launched just one product flavour with one active ingredient when it probably should have been a whole line with different flavours. Maybe the idea could have been tried with a different brand and some more advertising. We just weren't successful in getting enough buy-in from the marketing folks, who saw the popsicle as a small line extension rather than a new technology platform – we undersold it. The truth is that parents will spend more on kids' products than on themselves if the product works to help their kids, but we just didn't get behind it enough or explore it before we gave up.

Often we know in our gut that something is a good idea but when management and marketing don't want to push it, we have to give up some good ideas. As an R&D person it is really hard, as you can't fall on your sword for every good idea.

Dennis Nelson, Former R&D Director, Pfizer

b

Summary

>——▶ **Challenge the channel to market early** – Do not be fooled into thinking that the normal core channels can and will automatically push a new product or service, nor that the customer contact centre is best placed to service it.

>——▶ **Do not underestimate which new capabilities are needed or how hard they are to acquire and leverage** – New capabilities take time to put in place, whether building from scratch or using third parties. Understand the role of the capabilities and allow time to develop them.

>——▶ **Ensure any brand development has a halo effect on the corporate as well as supporting the new proposition** – Positioning the new product or service within the overall

brand hierarchy needs to support both the product and the core brand. Otherwise, new brands come into play.

➤ **Check everything: the devil really is in the detail** – Understand the detail, particularly around the key assumptions, as early as possible.

➤ **Proactively manage the risks that matter** – Focus on a handful of key implementation risks and, above all else, manage the big risks of impacting the core brand and core investment profile.

➤ **Use beta phases to learn and adapt in the live market** – Use pilots to test and learn in a real market, but make sure there is rapid feedback on the KPIs in place before starting pilots. Where possible grow pilots to good scale to minimise launch risks.

➤ **The actual launch for a new product needs careful planning** –Think carefully about launch timing from a corporate perspective as well as that of the new product.

➤ **Invest enough to win** – Make sure sufficient investment is put in to give the new business a fighting chance. We never know how well a new venture will do, but withholding the required investment for it to compete properly limits its chances significantly.

Sustaining
Innovation

Section C

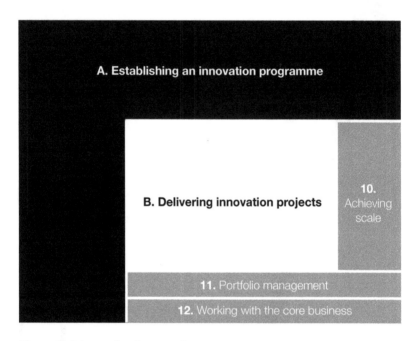

Figure C.1: Innovation framework

Delivering a single innovation project can be incredibly tough (albeit also incredibly rewarding). Sustaining an ongoing programme of innovation projects can be even more challenging.

If the programme has been established correctly and there is a good flow of projects then it should be sustainable. Nevertheless, long-term success requires an additional set of management and leadership skills, as set out in this final section.

Figure C.1 shows a modified version of the innovation framework diagram, with section C on sustaining innovation broken down into its principal constituent areas.

The chapters of Section C discuss these sub-sections within sustaining innovation.

10. Achieving Scale

Don't fire and forget – ongoing effort is required to achieve scale.

Launching a new product or service is not the end of the story. It often requires nurturing and further pivoting as staff and customers alike learn about it. Unless you have hit one of those rare overnight success stories, a lot of work is still required. Messaging will need to be refreshed, new features that did not make the launch proposition should be added and operational processes need to be standardised.

Harder still, rarely are the core business stakeholders prepared for a further period of learning and improving. Rather, they can change from being understanding and forgiving supporters of the project to demanding stakeholders expecting to see results – specifically positive financial results.

Laying the groundwork for this period by continuing to communicate in terms of piloting and testing rather than launching can help, but fundamentally the finance director is going to be looking for numbers. The good news is that there are ways of driving scale into a new venture, as set out below.

An inherent potential to scale

The potential for scaling a venture needs to be fully understood right from the start. One of the selection questions for prioritising opportunities at the very beginning should be the ability to scale, as highlighted in chapter 6. Then, throughout the design phase, it is necessary to be thinking not just about how to test and prove the minimum viable proposition, but also to understand what the operating model will look like at scale and what the roadmap is to get there.

Case example: Choosing the right projects for scaling at Barclays

You need to consider scalability early, both from a market perspective but also by understanding the delivery model. Here at Barclays, Pingit is a great example of something that was simple and cheap, a fairly basic financial concept that appeals to a wide audience with good usability, and was easily scalable.

However, I've seen other projects, which have been great ideas and even gone through to trial in the market and perform well for customers, but then can't be rolled out as the reality of investing in new infrastructure or technology in a launch context is far beyond delivering a small trial. You have to think through what would happen next after the trial, what the roadmap looks like and the delivery route for rolling it out.

Andrew Harris, Director of Deposits, Barclaycard

Case example: Preparing for scale at RWE npower

The plans for scale need to be embedded into the launch plan. It should already have been thought about on the roadmap. Part of the point of doing a Proof of Concept is to understand how the infrastructure will scale.

At RWE npower we piloted in Newcastle with a carved out call centre team and franchised and liveried engineers. Apart from testing the service and proposition, the reason was to understand the scaling challenges and we worked out that the only way to do it would be to acquire through M&A. The decision is already made before you launch. We already had deals done with the boiler and parts supplier to be ready for scale. That meant that when we advertised on TV with the Wallace and Gromit advertising and the floodgates opened, we were ready for it and had a proven model. You have to design a mature version of the operating model and scale it back for the pilot, but keep the mature one up your sleeve ready for when the business really starts to take off.

Gideon Hyde, Co-Founder & Partner, Market Gravity

Opportunities provided by open innovation

In some cases, an open innovation approach can drive scale and improve the commercial case. Partner companies may provide access to new customers and channels, greater efficiencies and shared investment costs. Likewise, when dealing with digital ventures, a single product can often be turned into a platform and multiple product offering using the API approach as per the Orange case example below. In this way, one product can be turned into multiple products, each with associated revenues, and it can drive new revenue streams such as platform fees.

Case example: Open innovation improving business distribution at Orange

Every innovation project I design, I include APIs. If I can, I design the product on top of an API so it becomes just one example of how to use the API. Then others can build other products around it which can make a win-win for business: we give you the tools and you create. Each service created on top of your APIs distribute your business to untapped markets: one stone, multiple birds.

Apart from making the idea bigger, it enables entrepreneurs to build services and generate new revenues from the end customer. They are happy as no up front cost is required, and we've both made money as the revenue is shared.

The role of the designer or innovation manager is then to create platforms and toolkit that will help others to design: I'm not selling you a service, I'm selling you the ability to build your own.

Often we build APIs with limited capacity that are available for free to entrepreneurs. When large corporates want something more scalable, with higher service level, or more features, then we charge a flat fee for the API. Developers' feedback helps us build the API and make it strong and corps are paying for these improvements. It's about developing the eco-system in a virtuous circle for every participant.

Nicolas Bry, SVP Innovation, Orange Vallée

Incentivise the team with the right targets

Financial targets can encourage the wrong behaviours once a project is launched and it is important to choose targets wisely so that they push the team to deliver the right performance. You get what you measure, so you need to put in place the right targets. Often new ventures are signed off on the basis of having significant long-term growth potential, yet teams may well then be managed on their profit performance in the first year. This can create the wrong focus and undermine and even destroy a venture, as in the support services case study below.

Case example: Ill-chosen incentives and short-termism kill venture at a support services company

Following a large innovation programme at the height of the dot.com boom in the late 90s, the board decided to pursue a project that would take the company's security division into the internet consumer shopping space. An impressive secure shopping portal was created that delivered an experience close to Amazon's current 'one-click' system and was very secure. Big retail partners were signed up, and the project trialled successfully with great feedback so the launch plan was approved with strong expectations.

The business model was based on scale and required strong growth in users in the first few years to deliver long-term gains. To this end, the business case allowed for significant investment in marketing and cautious profit figures in the early years.

It all went wrong when the team newly appointed to run the project were incentivised on hitting these cautious profit targets, which might sound reasonable, but led to the wrong behaviours, once under pressure.

Whilst at first the team tried to follow the business plan of investing heavily in marketing to attract users to the website, there were soon budget challenges elsewhere in the business that applied pressure to the venture team. The venture team then realised that they could cut spending on marketing and make significant savings, so significant in fact that all they had to do was cut the marketing spend and they could still hit their profitability targets and so meet their bonus target. Unsurprisingly, without the marketing spend, the portal never acquired the required user numbers and the project died whilst the venture team walked away with their bonus. Who knows if the venture would ever have succeeded in the fast-changing world of e-tail, but these incentives combined with short-termism from the business meant it never stood a chance.

Dan Taylor, Managing Director North America, Market Gravity

Obviously, teams need to be managed against the business case targets, but business cases for new ventures never reflect reality and so, far more important than year one cost and revenue figures, is performance around measures such as customer satisfaction, repeat usage and purchase, referrals, customer growth and retention, the ability to adapt and improve against these measures, and an ongoing focus in the long-term vision. The focus should still be on testing, learning and improving the proposition.

Summary

⋙⟶ **Propositions need to have an inherent potential to scale** – Understand what would need to be true to scale an idea from the start, and whether this is plausible.

⋙⟶ **Open innovation provides opportunities for increasing the scale of opportunity** – Consider how partners and other 'open' approaches can drive scale more quickly.

⋙⟶ **You get what you measure** – Target and incentivise the team against the right objectives. Ensure incentives and objectives are aligned to scale rather than short-term performance.

11. Portfolio Management

Proactively manage the programme as a whole to maximise chances of success.

> "I put 90% of my focus against breakthrough ideas. Incremental innovation is just a cost of doing business. It doesn't change the trajectory but you need it to keep everybody happy. Pushing for breakthrough may mean 6-7 misses before a big win, but that is why we're here."
>
> **Shannon Bryan, GM Customer Strategy and Planning, Shell**

Do not unwittingly apply a shotgun approach

Innovation theory often stresses the importance of developing a portfolio of new ideas to spread risk and improve the chances of success. As highlighted in chapter 1, research suggests that on average it takes 3,000 raw ideas to deliver one commercial success, and this type of ratio is often quoted when discussing portfolio management. It leads many companies to develop a large pipeline of ideas.

It is certainly true that many ideas fail, either whilst still in development or soon after launch and therefore backing multiple projects does enhance the chances of at least one of them succeeding. We never know which ideas will succeed and which will fail; if we did, we would all be millionaires as we would just be able to back successful ideas from the beginning. Even then, great ideas can fail, and often do, and so we invest in as many apparently good ideas as we can.

Case example: Understanding the failure rate at Barclays

Often, the reality of new products is so far from assumptions in a business case, that rather than continue to test, learn and adapt, projects just get canned and, worse still, stakeholders start to lose faith in the numbers and research carried out.

Here at Barclays, we understand that for banking in the digital age we have to be more like a technology company and need to think that way and understand innovation and the associated failure rates; invest in a hundred projects to get one real success. You can't look for a single slam dunk to invest in, and expect to be right every time. Instead, we ring-fence some cash to try lots of projects.

Andrew Harris, Director of Deposits, Barclaycard

What is less often considered about this approach is the level of focus required to turn an idea into a successful launch. It may take a year or even more of hard work for a raw idea to be developed, tested and iterated, culminating in a potentially expensive full launch. Along the way, there are many pitfalls to avoid and barriers to overcome. When multiple projects in a portfolio are being worked on, each one can suffer from a lack of individual focus. Different projects may have conflicting requirements from systems or operations, or need prioritisation to acquire development resource. The sheer workload and complexity of the projects can lead innovation teams to burn out, and innovation leaders may struggle to give sufficient time and focus to individual projects.

" Innovation leaders should think again
about trying to invest in
as many good ideas as possible
and instead work on a smaller
portfolio that they can
be dedicated to. "

Case example: Focusing the portfolio and pipeline at Xerox

We are pretty methodical with trying to manage a balanced portfolio of projects in our pipeline with 1/3 of opportunities in explore, 1/3 in incubate and 1/3 in partner. It's important to maintain a good balance in the portfolio especially as you move solutions into partner and get absorbed with commercialization efforts. You need to have enough ideas coming in the door to allow for the ones that fall out or fail fast. At Xerox we maintain a home-grown system where we track:

1. Business case

2. Yields (including impact on other deals that we might win that our innovation will be part of)

3. Customer contact – customer screening sessions, event speaking etc.

Also, we pull the CIOs together regularly across our service industry & capabilities verticals (Healthcare, Transport, HR, Education, Customer care, Print & Transactions etc...). Typically, we devote a ½ day each month to review our pipeline and deep dive into an industry for full business case reviews. In addition we invite outside speakers & business partners to address topics that align with our business strategy. We do the same with the researchers. This is important as connecting the dots and creating dialogue between innovation & research across industries can uncover innovation *lift* within the corporation that might have applicability to your industry.

It's important to keep your pipeline manageable. When we started our journey in innovation 5 years ago on the services side we were too ambitious with too many projects in the pipeline relative to what the team could focus on. Our call for projects typically starts six months prior to the New Year with a simple two page business case submission from the business side and researchers. This then goes into a review and bidding process that lasts until November. During that time we fine tune the proposals for our pipeline with the lines of business relative to strategic alignment, the total addressable market and potential of the opportunity delivery relative to our customers unmet needs and our internal resources. This vetting process has a lot of back and forth discussion between the business groups and the research group. While the process is time consuming it's similar to what one undergoes in budgeting and forecasting running a business unit.

Denise Fletcher, Chief Innovation Officer, Healthcare & Pharma, Xerox

A robust programme management function can help, but teams can still easily become overstretched. In this context, the role of the leadership and support network becomes imperative to drive clarity and focus, but most importantly, innovation leaders should think again about trying to invest in as many good ideas as possible, and instead work on a smaller portfolio that they can be dedicated to. In this way, a small number of the very best ideas can be nurtured properly with greater chance of hitting the target. Managing the portfolio against the purpose of the innovation programme can help to maintain this focus and ensure the programme is working on the right areas of innovation.

It is not just the innovation programme itself which tends to suffer from portfolio management challenges. Many businesses struggle to keep on top of their core portfolio of live products. Variants based on old versions, models or customers on specific packages due to sales promotions can create significant complexity, even within an apparently simple product portfolio. An innovation programme can benefit from reviewing the core portfolio as a means of identifying gaps and opportunities in the current offerings, and as a way of understanding the customer approach to decision-making during the purchase process.

C

Sustaining Innovation

Case example: Focusing the portfolio around three targets at Cancer Research UK

I love the simple three target portfolio and can arrange the themes around it:

1. Tactical – Easy, quick innovations, often around customer experience.

2. Strategic – Typically, new customers or channels.

3. Disruptive – Step-change innovation like new business models, adjacencies.

For example, at Cancer Research UK, Genes in Space (an online game which analyses real patient data from new treatments as users play it) was a great success that could absolutely step-change the development time for new drugs, whereas the Dryathlon (a campaign encouraging men to give up alcohol for one month in aid of Cancer Research) focused on men as a new customer segment, and then you have something like no-make-up-selfies – a tactical innovation that comes from an agile and responsive team.

Tim Thorne, Former Innovation Director, Cancer Research UK

Sometimes a portfolio can be too broad. Often companies may have grown through acquisition and have multiple overlapping products, sometimes on different legacy systems, and removing legacy products from a portfolio is rarely done as it feels like a lot of hard work for no real new innovation. Yet, managing, marketing and selling so many products can be costly and resource intensive. Simplifying the portfolio may release resource for new innovation and create a clear platform for new growth opportunities as well as creating a better and simpler experience for customers. It's not always the right thing to do to look to launch new products if the portfolio is already overly complex.

Case example: Simplifying the portfolio at E.ON UK

When designing a new tariff that aimed to simplify the energy-buying process for customers, we found that a number of variants, such as customer meter type and in what part of the country they lived, made the proposition incredibly hard to deliver and communicate as it fundamentally was complex. Whilst working on this set-back we also decided to look at what these variants meant for the portfolio. It turned out that the company had over 14,000 product and price variations. This was an energy company that essentially measures and bills customers for the amount of electricity they use. So simple, yet there were over 14,000 variations for different customers. Whilst a number of these variant types were hard to remove we set out on a whole new path to simplify the portfolio, both for customers to understand but also for the company to manage. Over time, thousands of these variations were eliminated and whilst there are still more than you would like, the improvement in customer experience has been immense.

Dan Taylor, Managing Director North America, Market Gravity

Monitor key metrics to improve the programme

Innovation requires significant resources, which come in the form of staff salaries, research costs, investments in the innovations themselves, and the time and focus that is required from the leadership team. These costs, together with the strategic importance of most innovation programmes, make it imperative that they be properly measured and evaluated. However, this can be difficult as innovation teams are continually adapting and changing direction, meaning that objectives and targets can become obsolete quickly.

Too often, companies simply monitor individual projects rather than the innovation programme as a whole, which fails to present a full and accurate picture. Measuring return on investment (ROI) on an innovation programme can become cloudy as debates rage over whether to measure each innovation project individually or whether to add in all the broader overhead costs of the innovation programme itself, which may well create a negative picture of the overall programme and of individually successful projects within it too. Normally, innovation programmes are commercially driven and need to add to the bottom line. To that end, whichever approach a company uses, the financial performance cannot be ignored and has to be the key indicator of success or failure.

Some companies try to set high-level company targets such as '20% of revenues need to come from products launched in the last three years'. These can cover the direct costs and benefits of the new product, but also the indirect ones where the proposition may impact broader customer service costs or customer satisfaction and hence retention benefits. Other companies try to go beyond this to look at both hard financial benefits and soft intangible benefits, such as brand perception and employee engagement.

Given the future focus and the difficulty of measuring the outputs, innovation programmes are an area where measuring inputs can also be helpful. For example, monitoring the volume of opportunities in the pipeline and, importantly, the speed at which they are progressing through the pipeline, can be an important indicator. These inputs cannot necessarily show that you will successfully hit the desired outputs, but they can show if you definitely will not (i.e. if there are too few/small opportunities progressing too slowly). Some companies measure both inputs and outputs of an innovation programme, such as Tata, which has developed a tool, the Innometer, which looks to monitor and evaluate the results of the programme and also many other factors – such as the process and culture – in order to identify where and when interventions are required.

Case example: Broader measures of success at BT

You have to be really candid about this from the start. People hugely over-estimate the short-term impact of innovation. BT never really had a balance sheet for the intangibles like reputation and brand value. Externally, BT Click&Buy was a huge success, we won the Grand Prix at the New Media Age awards and our reputation for being innovative was really good as a result – but internally we were just beaten up for missing the numbers.

Ian Price, Former CEO, BT Click&Buy, BT

The right approach will vary from company to company based on the purpose and objectives of the overall innovation programme and the culture of the organisation, but the important thing is for companies to find a consistent and objective way of monitoring the performance of the innovation programme as a whole rather than just individual projects.

Leverage staff experience to embed learning from both successes and failures

This book itself is trying to capture innovation lessons, and all of the suggested approaches and advice are based on real experience of both successful and failed projects, but these will still only serve as lessons if they are put into practice in other projects. Sadly, whilst many projects do terminate with a team review of the things that worked well and those that did not, very rarely are these insights proactively applied to similar situations in other projects.

Case example: Perception of failure vs learning the lessons at NBC

At NBC, we were thinking of a series of web-only TV shows which would be interactive and begin to join up TV and digital. So we trialled the idea with three shows which went well, especially one covering the war in Syria where we had access to a refugee camp and we allowed direct access by Twitter for people to ask questions to those in the refugee camp.

On the back of these three we decided to do one on the back of the nightly news programme so that at the end of the programme people would switch to this news extra show on the web. There was a technical glitch with promoting it during the show, but even without that the conversion to getting viewers to the web show was unspectacular. So it was seen as a failure, though I think it was actually hugely useful, it showed that the people are too busy watching TV in the evenings to switch over and watch more news on the web. The failure would have been to not try it and not to learn.

Julian March, SVP Editorial and Innovation, NBC News

The truth is that such lessons are often a personal journey for the individuals involved and it can be incredibly hard for others to capture the lessons, understand them and then apply them to their own work. The implication of this is that retention and consistency of personnel in the programme becomes very important, as evidenced by the Virgin example below.

Case example: Staff retention enabling learning at Virgin Atlantic

Virgin had good staff retention. That meant that whilst the codification process didn't really happen, many of the learnings were personal and the same teams would move on to the next project and so the same mistakes would not be made again. It speeded up as people knew where the dead-ends were and the short-cuts. This meant that the first seat project took four years, but every subsequent project we delivered was far quicker than that.

Joe Ferry, Former Head of Design, Virgin Atlantic

Continually reinvigorate the team with fresh talent

One of the challenges with managing an innovation team is keeping the thinking fresh. If the individuals stay in the team for a number of years then ideas, energy and approaches are all in danger of going stale.

Even from the very start, it is not unusual for corporates to seek external recruits for innovation teams, believing that their current staff are stuck in their ways and not creative. There is definitely merit in including external recruits, not solely for acquiring the right skill sets and attitudes, but also to give a diverse range of experience from other companies and industries. However, this should be balanced with internal recruits. Deep knowledge of the core organisation, stakeholders, politics and culture will be important, and many existing employees may well have the right attributes for innovation, but they are just either hidden or not expected to express them in their current roles.

Innovation can be a specialist career for many that can be quite different from other professions. For example, in most job interviews you might have some reservations about a candidate who moved jobs every two or three years, never settling you might think, but that is the classic path for intrapreneurs. In this way, it is a surprise that innovation is rarely recognised as a specialist career either by HR departments or by recruitment agencies.

Some companies manage this challenge proactively by rotating appropriate staff through the innovation function. This brings benefits of keeping thinking fresh and ensuring ever-changing perspectives due to the in-built diversity. It also gets more people across the organisation involved in the innovation process and they are likely to become advocates once back in their own functions.

At the same time, it comes with a number of challenges and risks. Sometimes it can be seen as a stepping stone for exit from the company, either because the employee does not want to return to their day job after experiencing an entrepreneurial culture or because it becomes a harbour for people wanting to leave anyway – which is unlikely to be best for the innovation team. Likewise, this approach puts at risk having innovation specialists that are highlighted above, so careful thought needs to be given to how rotation is done and how to balance it with permanent staff.

Case example: Team rotation at NBC

You have to institutionalize the test and learn approach and get the cycle as fast and tight as possible. I really like the idea of setting up a spike unit with a team of four people who would focus on innovating around priority issues defined by the business units. You'd run it on rotation so that people move in and out every three months on a staggered timeline. So every three weeks, one of the four moves on. They then take the lessons back with them.

Julian March, SVP, Editorial & Innovation at NBC News

Given that by nature many entrepreneurs are always looking for the next challenge or big idea, talent management and succession planning in an innovation team is one of the biggest risks, yet rarely is it properly considered let alone fully addressed. Typically, innovation teams will be small both because of available investment and because small teams tend to be more effective. This implies that there are just a few people who will be critical to the success of individual projects and they will live and breathe a project. At the same time, these people are naturally ambitious and sought after in the market, which can lead to a high staff turnover rate. In some ways this is a good thing, as a successful innovation team will benefit from regular injections of new blood to stop the environment becoming stale, but it also leads to the issue of managing resourcing to ensure projects are not impacted by staff turnover.

Any good HR function will ensure that succession plans are in place, but given the importance of these individuals to specific projects a number of actions are required. First is to ensure a strong cross-functional team working closely together, so that no single individual is solely working on a certain aspect of the venture. The whole team should be engaged in and up-to-date with a number of work-streams so that they are able to continue to drive it forwards in the event of one of the team leaving the project for whatever reason. This issue is even more serious when it relates to the innovation leader, but a similar approach of ensuring project accountability is held by a range of individuals across the programme can reduce risk.

Case example: Managing team transitions in healthcare giants

At Warner-Lambert, we were working on a new snack product that looked really promising. The customer research was excellent, with great feedback from the prototype and lots of time and effort went in to getting the product a long way through the process. Then the Category Director was replaced by somebody else who decided not to focus on snacks and killed the project.

This is very common and you need to mitigate succession by having a product portfolio that is owned upward and by multiple functions rather than just one individual. For example at Pfizer, we operated global category management with representatives from the category from each region and the R&D team. They agreed together which products to focus on and sold them into the Divisional Leadership team. If one person changed, it was much less likely to derail the programme.

The more you formalize the team and leadership with process the less likely that things will change for idiosyncratic or political reasons. You can't eliminate politics but you can help mitigate it through process.

Priorities and projects should be owned by groups of stakeholders and institutionalized. They should be championed and administered by people who are as neutral and as close to the customer as possible.

Arthur Fox, Founder, Innovation Global Network

Summary

➤ **Most businesses unwittingly apply a shotgun approach to portfolio management for innovation projects** – Rather than trying to push many projects through to improve the probability of success, focus your effort and resource on a few of the very best ideas and give them the best chance.

➤ **Measuring success is complex, but monitoring key metrics can help improve the programme** – Measure the overall programme as well as individual projects and use metrics that align to the purpose and vision of the programme.

➤ **Leverage staff experience to embed learning from both successes and failures** – Lessons from success and failure are only valuable if put into practice on future projects. The most effective way of doing this is maintaining a core team and bringing their experience to bear on projects across the portfolio.

➤ **Continually reinvigorate the team with fresh talent** – Proactively manage staff turnover and rotation to balance experience in the team with fresh thinking and ambition.

12. Working With The Core Business

Proactively defend innovation against short-termism

Despite the advent of lean and agile methodologies and the ability to rapid prototype pretty much anything in almost any industry, innovation still takes time. From all the upfront work to establish a programme before you have even started looking at ideas, and then actually identifying, developing and testing the opportunities themselves, it can often take at least 12 months to get new innovations to market and then the business will have to be grown from a handful of pilot customers to a number that is meaningful for the core business – a task which can take years.

Case example: Understanding how long it can take to become established in a new market at E.ON UK

The error is in thinking that this is easy. The belief that you think you can crack a market in two years, not understanding that real retailing is a tough business and that you will make mistakes and need to learn. This gets interpreted as incompetency and that the business is not good at this so they change tack, when it actually needs years to build a new area.

There is an oil major who moves into new markets and they have a saying that, 'after ten years, you start to know what you're doing, and after 20 years you start to feel comfortable.' Well, I've seen people expect to know what you're doing and be comfortable after three years!

WhisperGen would be an example. We spent ages getting a trustworthy product, because it takes time to develop the capability and product. Even if you discount a product like WhisperGen as there were additional challenges around the technology, the same is still true of other markets like Solar PV, where the technology is bulletproof, but it still takes time and you need the staying power to see it through. Of course this issue can be exacerbated by changes in the strategy. Sometimes, strategy can change quicker than innovation can deliver. A new product may have a gestation of five years and there is only a strategic focus of three years, so the business is just not prepared to stay in it for the long term.

Charles Bradshaw-Smith, Former Head of Innovation, E.ON

Case example: Understanding the innovation timeframe at Evonik

We were trying to promote some new product ideas. We had a technology with great potential for certain industry applications based around a smarter chemical delivery system. It's not a totally new idea in itself but the solution was great, but to demonstrate the commercial potential it needs testing and regulatory approval and you need an industry and final-user partners to do that. So it's a long process, and that's after you've synthesized the molecule and tested it and so on. But the moment you show realistic timeframes to the business, there is not much stomach for it.

I'm trying to grow an innovation platform, but the business has a one to three year timeframe, which just isn't realistic for radical innovation.

Sanjay Gupta, VP & Regional Head of Corporate Innovation Strategy & Management Division, Evonik

---

Case example: Quick wins to gain sponsorship at MetLife

There is a danger zone, where there is lots of activity but it then takes time to get results. You have to try to get small wins and earn credit. So much depends on the sponsor and support. For example, we ran a social campaign in a small country in one of regions that just focused on resolving some customer issues. This showed we could get real excitement from customers who not only co-created some of the ideas but also helped choose which ideas to pursue. This got great customer feedback and gained us the trust and sponsorship from the regional head. Then he invited us to focus one of his big leadership meetings on innovation. The ideas from that got great buy-in with that sponsorship and one of them went on to be launched and is now the best performing proposition in the region.

Terrance Luciani, VP, Innovation, MetLife

Unfortunately, it is rare for an innovation team to be afforded such time to deliver meaningful revenues. Often the innovation programme was established due to specific market pressures in the first place and the core normally needs a quick response. There is a risk that the burning platform just burns down.

This pressure often comes in the form of budget cuts as the organisation seeks to maintain profits, and the innovation team can often be one of the first targets for such cuts. Alternatively, a change of leadership or strategic direction can also put a swift end to an innovation programme unless it can clearly demonstrate tangible value to the organisation. If the original burning platform was real, then the programme should remain valid through some organisational challenges, but nevertheless the pressure can often take a significant toll.

Case example: Not delivering revenues fast enough at Powergen/E.ON UK

The Powergen venture unit, Spark, had strong top-level sponsorship. The CEO got behind it and knew what he had bought into, particularly when compared to other programmes I have seen where they get going quickly but as soon as they need to scale and draw upon significant corporate resources find that the whole top team had never properly 'got it'.

Spark had clear objectives around both culture change and new revenue streams; we got some early wins with the roadshows that were trying to portray a different Powergen, a vision beyond a simple risk-averse utility. We set up a good infrastructure and we didn't try to do it all ourselves. We had what felt like a good balance of a strong internally recruited team together with the necessary skills from external consultants. It felt like we were seen to be successful before we had delivered any new revenues.

However, at the end of the day, when change at the top came we had been too slow to deliver revenues. E.ON had their own unit in Germany investing in promising technology start-ups and were used to a portfolio of ventures which already had protectable IP and were largely post-revenue. We did not successfully make the case for our approach within E.ON Ventures and for a Powergen management team in the process of being acquired, protecting a cash consuming venture unit was never going to be high on the priority list.

Whether a global company with a very strong utility strategy would ever have accepted a venture unit in one of its national subsidiaries is questionable, but if we had got the big ideas off the ground faster and demonstrated value earlier we would certainly have been in a stronger position. We were focused on building big long-term businesses capable of attracting external investors, rather than generating early revenues. Three years is just too long in a corporate, and in our case was longer than the tenure of our board sponsors. When E.ON acquired Powergen, the new UK management team shut down the unit, maintaining only a small number of close-to-core teams.

Gary Marsh, Former Associate Director, E.ON Power Technologies

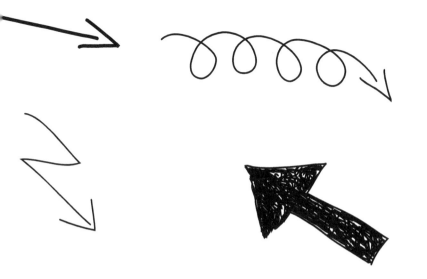

ffIt is necessary to identify and deliver **some projects that bring** quick commercial benefits **to allow breathing space** for larger developments. **JJ**

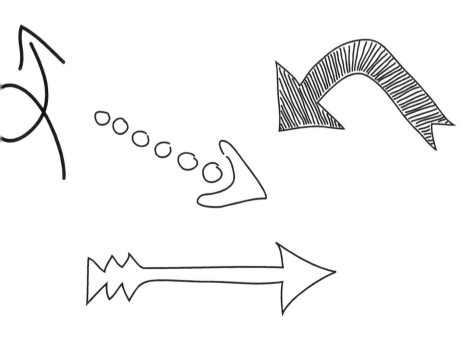

With this in mind, it is necessary to identify and deliver some projects that bring quick commercial benefits to allow breathing space for the larger developments. These do not need to be big, but they need to show that the team can deliver and should drive enough value to pay for the programme.

Case example: Delivering quick wins at the Carbon Trust

You have to get early successes. We started a Low Carbon consultancy business. It wasn't exciting or with massive potential but it did have potential to get going quickly and be a cash cow – a people business that was asset light could get early cash flow. As we've found as an independent start-up, once you get the cash flow to cover the cost of the team, then it's harder to get rid of you. It costs the company money to close you down. An operating budget can be cut very easily so you need something to keep you alive.

Andrew Wordsworth, Former MD, Carbon Trust Enterprises

Another approach is to gain public commitment to the programme at an early stage. Once shareholders have been told that the organisation is investing in something, it is a little bit harder to withdraw the funding.

One final tactic is to make sure that the team are responsible for the P&L of early stage ventures as well as generating and developing ideas. This way there is a real business that needs managing rather than just a central overhead, and it is far harder to cull a team.

"Everybody defaults to short-termism as soon as the going gets tough. The answer for me is in portfolio management. Don't have a department that is just responsible for the front end, they have to run at least some ideas through to execution. Otherwise they're seen as just paper-pushers and fluffy ideas people. If the going gets tough, they should be able to focus on the in-life projects and then back into more creative stuff when the time is right. They have to be accountable for delivery as well."

Michael Johnson, Former MD New Ventures, Which?

Build positive relations with the core business

Executive sponsorship may be sufficient to establish an innovation programme, but to be enduring, it needs to drive success in the core organisation too. This often means finding parts of the business that will benefit from individual projects and working with them to deliver success for the core business as well as for the innovation project.

Case example: Finding the win-win at British Gas

If you're asking the business to open up their marketing channel for you, there is naturally huge resistance as people are targeted on their own things. There is channel and resource contention and problems with budget allocation, but you have to give the new team the oxygen to succeed. We tried a more directive approach with the CEO telling divisional leaders to support the business, but as soon as it gets a layer or two down it still gets bogged down in the same issues. You need the win-win – so we focused every project on retention or acquisition or cost reduction for the existing business. Telling them solar was a new and exciting business was pointless, but telling them that free insulation to existing customers would give an x% uptick in brand loyalty and a corresponding y% decline in churn then suddenly you'd get a lot of support.

Gearoid Lane, Former Managing Director, British Gas New Markets

It is also important that the purpose and excitement flow through the heart of a business at all levels. This means extensive internal communications programmes to bring the programme to life for other members of staff all around the business and help them to understand its importance and how they can be involved. Employee engagement innovation programmes can be useful in achieving this goal, although there are all sorts of other possible approaches, from roadshows to all-staff meetings. Just telling staff about it is rarely enough – there need to be ways for them to be involved and the opportunity for them to benefit from the programme too.

Case example: Helping the core to innovate at Boehringer Ingelheim

We've been good on communications, like using the intranet and Yammer as a social media platform that quickly had 10,000 employees using it worldwide and it became the unofficial place to go for contacts and information. I have loads of followers on that platform which helps get the message out.

We run success stories, and webcasts and also a disruptive innovation series where we offer workshops looking for new business models and fresh ideas. The most important thing is knowing who the innovators are around the business and it may not be in their job title. Once you have that network, you find synergies and grow ideas together that would not have made it otherwise.

Stephan Klaschka, Director, Global Innovation Management, Boehringer Ingelheim

Be ready to integrate back into the core business

I have emphasised the importance of keeping new ventures separate from the core organisation throughout their development. However, there comes a point once they are live in the market that they need to be managed like a mature business and realise the benefits of the corporate scale.

Integrating young ventures back into the core business can be risky and many companies are wary about doing this before the venture is standing firmly on its own two feet. However, there can be benefits from an early integration, such as an enhanced commercial focus and greater operational expertise and support. To this end, the venture should be at a position where the company has made a definite decision to back it, based on the post-launch lessons, so that integration effort is not wasted on a potential failure, but it can still be done before the venture is fully established or has broken even.

With this in mind, one of the key tasks of the corporate entrepreneur is to understand the needs of the various divisions of the core business in order to find where support may lie for a project and where its eventual home may be once it is stable. It is common to focus on the changes required to the core and the challenges involved when delivering an innovation project, yet many projects can also create benefits for the core, be it fewer calls to a contact centre or improved loyalty. Working with the core to ensure these win-win benefits are fully delivered can be an important step in gaining proactive support for an innovation project at any stage.

C

Case example: Developing innovation outside the core, ready for future integration at British Gas

We got frustrated trying to leverage the corporate resource. At first we said let's not build our own fleet, supply chain, IT and so on as it's all available in the core, but we learnt to ignore all of the internal capabilities as they have their own annual objectives and targets and you are just a distraction.

You can't underestimate the importance of doing a reality check and constantly applying it. Do you really have the right to win that, you think? You might talk about leveraging the customer access, distribution channels or brand to win but the question is 'Really?' It just won't happen in practice. Working with the core is a real challenge and that's why this stuff normally happens in small businesses.

Now that I run my own small business, I dedicate 100% of my time to making money and growing the business. If I was still in a corporate, I'd spend 50% or more of my time in management meetings or other such corporate fluff. I think the best plan for a corporate might be to let a small company do the hard work and then acquire it! It's hard to build something better than a start-up would build it – lean, mean and 100% focused!

Gearoid Lane, Former Managing Director, British Gas New Markets

Summary

⇢ **Proactively defend innovation against short-termism** – Quick wins can extend the life of a programme long enough to develop the long-term opportunities.

⇢ **Building positive relations with the core business is a key element of sustainability of an innovation programme** – This means finding individual wins for core business leaders, where your projects can help solve some of their issues. It also means engaging the whole organisation to involve them in the programme.

→ **Be ready to integrate back into the core business** – There comes a point when many new businesses are strong enough to be managed as proper commercial entities and can benefit from the discipline and scale of the core organisation. Plan this transition early and work with the relevant part of the business to make it successful.

C

Sustaining Innovation

Conclusion

I have covered a lot of ground in understanding how to make an innovation programme successful. Delivering innovation in big business is immensely rewarding, but is also very tough and hopefully this book provides a useful reference guide and examples of how to practically achieve success.

Good luck!

Acknowledgements

I'd like to thank all of the contributors who gave their time and expertise:

Aaron Proietti	John Mitchell
Andreas Welsch	Jose Davila
Andrew Der	Julian March
Andrew Wordsworth	Lee Osborne
Andrew Harris	Mark Southern
Arthur Fox	Mary Ward
Benjamin Braun	Meldrum Duncan
Charles Bradshaw-Smith	Michael Johnson
Dave Wardle	Mike Fairman
Dean Keeling	Nancy Shea
Deborah Arcoleo	Nicolas Bry
Delia Dumitrescu	Paul Wylde
Denise Fletcher	Peter Haigh
Dennis Nelson	Phil Clarke
Emily Clark	Phil Kohler
Gary Marsh	Philip Brittan
Gearoid Lane	Richard Harding
Georgina Schiffers	Ruth Whitten
Gideon Hyde	Sandrine Desbarbieux
Ian Price	Sanjay Gupta
James Gamage	Sarah Gregory
Jaime Kalfus	Scott Burns
Jason Stanard	Shafik Saba
Jim Meadows	Shannon Bryan
Joe Ferry	Simon Brown

Simon Coley   Tim Sefton

Stephan Klaschka   Tim Thorne

Terrance Luciani   Tom Hobbs

The content for this book is almost exclusively based on interviews with the contributors named above combined with my own experience. That said, I have also taken inspiration from a number of books on related topics:

Blue Ocean Strategy by W. Chan Kim and Renee Mauborgne (Harvard Business School Press, 2005)

Change by Design by Tim Brown (HarperCollins, 2009)

Customers Included by Mark Hurst and Phil Terry (Creative Good, Inc., 2013)

Defying Gravity by Polly Courtney, with Peter Sayburn and Gideon Hyde (Matador, 2010)

Escape Velocity by Geoffrey A. Moore (HarperCollins, 2011)

The Innovator's Dilemma by Clayton M. Christensen (Harvard Business School Press, 1997)

The Lean Startup by Eric Ries (Crown Publishing Group, 2011)

The Other Side of Innovation by Vijay Govindarajan and Chris Trimble (Harvard Business School Press, 2010)

The Science of Serendipity by Matt Kingdon (John Wiley & Sons Ltd, 2012)

Finally, I'd like to thank my wife and family and the team at Market Gravity for their unlimited support in the writing of *The Secrets of Big Business Innovation*, and likewise to Polly Courtney and also the team at Harriman House for their great guidance and expertise in publishing it. Thank you.

Reference list of case examples

Index

Index

Lightning Source UK Ltd.
Milton Keynes UK
UKHW02f0451270618
324850UK00007B/292/P

9 780857 194640